Your Horse & Pony

GREATESTGUIDES

This is a **GREATEST**GUIDES title

Greatest Guides Limited, Woodstock, Bridge End, Warwick CV34 6PD, United Kingdom

www.greatestguides.com

Series created by Harshad Kotecha

Thanks everyone! Joanne would like to thank the following people for their help, time and support: Adrian Milledge, Jenny Millman BHSAI Int SM, Amanda McGinnigle BHSII, Tara May, Michaela Twite, Sarah Shephard, Louise Ryan, Amy Coote, Sarah Light, Gartmore Riding School, Liz Abbiss, Emma Butler, Claire O'Halloran, Roger & Tori Bostock.

Greatest Guides is committed to a sustainable future for our planet. This book is printed on paper certified by the Forest Stewardship Council.

Printed and bound in the United Kingdom

ISBN 978-1-907906-13-8

In memory of
Jean King and Malvern Batchelor

Contents

Foreword from Jodie Kidd...

It is said that horses are great levelers. They can lift you emotionally when you're feeling down, as well as literally bring you back down to earth if you become over-confident.

In fact, there are few hobbies that can rival the highs and lows of owning, caring for and riding a horse. Whether it's being up to your knees in mud on a cold and dark January morning inspecting the latest ripped rug with frozen fingers or winning your first rosette at the local show, there's nothing quite like that special bond between horse and rider/owner.

And I should know! Having looked after 30 horses at one stage – not to mention five dogs, four cats and five chickens – I, too, have experienced the rollercoaster ride of emotions that are part and parcel of horse ownership.

For me, nothing beats the exhilaration of galloping along a Caribbean beach or the thrills and spills of playing polo – being a member of Great Britain's winning team at the Women's World Championships was an unforgettable experience.

But equally, just being in the countryside surrounded by horses, mucking them out and getting dirt under my finger nails, is my greatest happiness.

And I've been lucky in that my modeling career has always enabled me to fund my horses – from the showjumpers I competed when I was a teenager to world class polo ponies. Horses always were, and still are – as I currently own a racehorse – my biggest inspiration.

If your bookshelves are anything like mine, heaving under the weight of horsey publications, there will always be room for little books like this one.

Whether you are a seasoned rider or just discovering the wonderful world of horses for the first time, there's something for everyone here. From plugging gaps in knowledge – it's ideal for that annual riding club quiz – to solving problems while helping you save time and money, *Your Horse & Pony* is an invaluable addition to every horse lover's library.

Happy riding everyone!

Jodie Kidd

Horsing Around

" Horses are like chocolates – one's just not enough. "

Katie Price

Chapter 1
Horsing Around

Owning a horse or pony is a huge commitment and responsibility, so it's important to ask yourself honestly if you can provide the necessary time, money, experience, knowledge and facilities. Remember, keeping a horse can sometimes feel like you're flushing money down the drain every day!

If you've answered yes, yes, yes, yes and yes, then the next step is to give some careful thought to where the animal will live – most people aren't lucky enough to own a plot with land and stables. Will you rent a field and shelter (when the fee is dependent on the size of the field or paddock) or place your horse in a boarding stable (America/Australia)/livery yard (UK), thereby paying someone else to care for your horse?

Living it up

If you opt to board your horse/place him at livery – where you pay the owner of the stables a weekly or monthly fee – decide which arrangement suits your horse and your lifestyle best…

1. Pasture board/grass livery: When the animal lives outdoors. Usually the cheapest arrangement, this is best suited to hardy, native types.

2. Self-board/DIY (do-it-yourself) livery: Whereby you rent a field and stable and do all the work – mucking out, grooming and feeding – yourself.

3. Part board/livery: Varies between establishments but is generally when some of the work is done by yourself, such as grooming and/or mucking out in the evenings or at weekends, while the rest is carried out by staff at the stables.

4. Working board/livery: If you keep your horse at a riding school, this can be quite a good way to keep costs down. Your horse is ridden by clients in lessons as payment towards his keep.

5. Full board/livery: The most expensive method. Everything – feed, bedding, sometimes turning out, bringing in and changing blankets/rugs – is provided by the stables. All you have to do is turn up and ride! In most areas of America, apart from the east, though, this often doesn't include grooming and riding, which are usually inclusive in the UK. This is a good arrangement for people who work long hours, to pay for their horse, and who don't have time to undertake stable duties before or after work, although the downside means you have less opportunity to build a bond together.

Born in the USA!

The term 'livery stable' traditionally has a different meaning in the US compared to that in the UK. Once a common sight in every American town, until the motor car rendered these establishments superfluous from 1910, a livery stable was where horses, teams and wagons could be hired or where privately-owned horses boarded on a short-term basis. Commonly attached to a hotel or boarding house, livery stables were often the scene of gambling, cockfighting and stag shows. In the UK, a livery stable or yard is where horses are kept and cared for in return for payment from the owner.

Aspects to consider

If you decide you want to entrust your horse's care to a professional place, here are some points to bear in mind when researching and checking out stables…

DO:

- List what's important to you and what would benefit your horse – if your horse is semi-retired, for instance, safe off-road riding for relaxing hacks might be more important than an arena, which would be useful for owners who plan to compete and need a dedicated safe space to school or practice dressage tests.

- Listen to word of mouth – stables with lazy staff, minimal facilities or poor customer relations tend to have a high turnover of clients and soon gain a bad reputation.

- Ensure the stables are run as a business, not a hobby or sideline – the former is more likely to treat you as a valued customer.

DON'T:

- Opt for an establishment where horses are stabled 24/7.

- Engage the services of inexperienced, unqualified staff.

- Choose a stables where staff have a cavalier attitude towards safety – there should be clear rules and/or obvious signs regarding:

  - the security of horses and equipment (for instance, reference to whether horses are branded/tattooed/freezemarked/identity chipped, tack marked with zip codes/post codes or the premises covered by video surveillance).

  - fire prevention, safety and evacuation procedure (with a strong emphasis on no smoking).

  - the close supervision of young children and dogs.

Selling points

So you've decided on how and where to keep your horse, what about obtaining one in the first place? Well, you can buy a horse from a private seller, dealer (a good place to find a variety of horses and ponies) or breeder, while auctions, sales and charities are also possible sources but should only be reserved for the very experienced horseperson.

When embarking on your equine search mission, never underestimate word of mouth and the local horsey network, such as owners, breeders, instructors, boarding stables/livery yards and riding schools. If there's a particular horse you like the look of that's not for sale, ask where the owner bought him – if he came from a stud or breeding farm, other horses by the same stallion or out of the same mare might be available.

Search tools

Study the horses for sale sections in local newspapers, riding club journals and local and national equestrian magazines; place wanted ads on the noticeboards of local stables, feed merchants, saddlers and riding schools; scour the Internet and flick through your local Yellow Pages or, in the UK, grab a copy of the British Equestrian Directory for a list of reputable breeders and dealers.

QUICK T!P
SCAMBUSTERS!

Check the contact details in adverts. If the same telephone number crops up time and time again, bear in mind that the seller is probably a dealer – even if they stated otherwise.

If selling your horse online, be aware of Internet-based scams. Watch out for would-be buyers contacting you via email, particularly if they are based overseas and are offering more than the selling price, to cover transportation costs. Scammers offer to send a cheque, which rarely arrives but bounces if it does. NEVER part with your horse until payment has completely cleared.

Points of view

Narrow down a list of possible horses to a final shortlist, and call the owners to establish whether the horse will be suitable for your needs after all. Unless you are experienced in handling and training horses, it's best to avoid a youngster. Be honest about your capabilities and realistic about what you want to achieve.

When arranging a 'test ride', ask the owner if it's OK for you to bring along a knowledgable friend – ideally, your riding instructor.

10 of the best

When viewing a horse, always remember to ask the owner these 10 important questions:

1. Is the horse sound?

2. Is he quiet to ride in all respects?

3. What has he done previously and would he be suitable for my particular requirements (leisure riding, jumping, etc)?

4. Does the horse have any bad habits ('stable vices' like weaving, crib-biting or windsucking) or failings I should know about, and has he ever bucked, reared or napped?

5. Is he good to catch, box, shoe and clip?

6. Does he hack out happily on his own, in company and in traffic, and has he ever spooked at anything (ie. tractors or flapping plastic bags)?

7. Any previous illnesses/injuries? Is he currently on any medication and why?

8. How long have you owned the horse and why is he for sale?

9. What's the horse like in the stable and is he OK turned out with both mares and geldings?

10. How often is he currently worked and what bit/s or gadget/s is he ridden in?

First impressions

View the horse in a natural light. Does he look well with an alert expression, bright eyes and a healthy bloom to his coat?

Check for obvious problems such as evidence of injuries, scars or conformational faults, and run your hands down his legs to feel for any lumps or bumps, which may indicate possible splints or weaknesses. Look for good feet – very important – which are well trimmed and shod with no signs of cracks, and ideally set at an angle of 45 degrees. Shoes should be worn evenly – more wear on the inside or outside, for instance, could indicate a problem with the horse's conformation or way of going.

Ask for the horse to be walked and trotted up and down in hand on a hard surface to check for soundness. Does he move freely and track up?

QUICK T!P
BEHIND THE SCENES
It's a good idea to see how the horse responds when tacked up, loaded into a trailer or truck, and in his stable, to check he is friendly and has no obvious bad habits. Ensure that he hasn't been denied water – one old trick is to dehydrate a horse to make him quieter and easier to ride.

In the saddle

Not only jump aboard yourself, but ask both the owner and your instructor to ride the horse. That way, you'll be able to see how the horse moves for both his regular rider and a stranger from the ground. Taking along your instructor also means you can ask for the unbiased opinion of someone whose knowledge and ability you trust, as well as have them acting as a witness should the sale go ahead.

Take your instructor's advice – if he or she suggests that they ride the horse first, then agree, as they are best placed to gauge what the horse is like to ride fresh, and whether he is cold-backed.

Ideally, face the horse with as many different situations as you can: ride him out on his own, in company, and in traffic, and take him past a few out of the ordinary obstacles or situations, such as a garbage bin lying on its side, a plastic bag, or a tractor, to see how he reacts. Will he go first or last and pass the stables without napping and trying to head for home? If you want him to jump, pop him over a fence or two. Finally, ask yourself if you are:

1. Able to stop the horse?

2. Able to steer him?

3. Happy and comfortable when aboard?

Questions, questions

Don't be afraid to ask seemingly obvious or stupid questions, or to ride the horse again at a different time on another day to get an overall picture.

Find out whether any equipment – such as a saddle, bridle and blankets/rugs – are included in the price, at an extra cost or not at all. Remember that the latter could greatly impact on your budget.

Video star

If you are trying several horses, ask a friend to video you riding each one so you can review your experiences once you get home, thereby helping you come to a more informed decision.

Decisions, decisions!

Never decide there and then, particularly if you feel under pressure to commit. Go home and think about the horse carefully, making a list of his good and bad points and weighing up the pros and cons.

If you still can't make up your mind, want to see how the horse will react in new or unfamiliar surroundings or be 100 per cent sure you're making the right decision, ask to have him on a week's trial or for a short loan period. Do get fully insured first, though, as the horse will be your responsibility.

QUICK T!P
AVOID LIKE THE PLAGUE...
... a horse that you can't sit on ... can't get on the bit ... scares you ... doesn't respond to your aids. And don't part with your hard-earned cash on the first horse you see!

Comfort zone

Unless you are very experienced, steer clear of buying a horse with a short neck – these are often very strong to ride, while horses with a long back, upright pasterns or hocks set out behind can give an uncomfortable ride.

Young at heart

If you've got the time and experience to buy a youngster, look for a good temperament with a nice eye and positive outlook – a generous horse that wants to work.

Other points to look for are a good topline and canter – the latter usually suggests the horse will be easier to train.

In addition, ensure the horse is viceless and you know his history. Look for evidence of bad habits, like crib-biting, by checking out the condition of the stable and door. If he is on different bedding to the other horses, ask why – he might have an allergy, be prone to lameness/foot problems or be a box walker.

The write move

Once you have decided to buy, ask for something in writing from the vendor confirming the horse is what they say it is. That way, both parties' positions are clear, and should any disputes arise in the future, you'll have some signed evidence to back up your claim.

Deal or no deal?

In the UK, your protection under the Sales of Goods Act 1979 is greater if you buy a horse from a dealer, as the sale is classed as a business transaction and means you are entitled to your money back if the horse has a problem that makes him unsuitable for the purpose you bought him.

A good dealer relies on reputation and if the horse has a physical or behavioral problem or does not suit you, they should offer to refund the purchase price or exchange/part-exchange the animal – providing you return him within a certain timeframe. However, don't agree to a dealer taking the horse back only on condition he sells it on for you – you, and not the dealer, could be sued by the next owner if you fail to disclose a problem.

You are not covered by the above Act at auctions or if you are buying privately – the law 'caveat emptor' (let the buyer beware) exists here, which means you must be able to prove that the vendor knew – or ought to have known – that the horse had a problem, and suing for breach of contract will take time, money and patience. At the end of the day, it'll be your word against theirs – unless you have anything in writing from the seller.

In America, sales-related lawsuits, particularly when a sale is not documented in a well-written contract, can be expensive and may well exceed the value of the horse.

Under the hammer

If you buy from a sale or auction in the UK, remember that horses are traditionally sold in guineas (one guinea = £1.05). While some sales deal in English pounds, they charge a buyer's premium of 10 per cent of the price (so a £1,200 horse becomes £1,320). If VAT is payable on the sale price, you need to factor that in too.

Sales force

At some sales, the proceeds are taped in case there's any future dispute over what's said. Listen carefully to the information the auctioneer gives out while the horse is in the ring as this may influence your decision on whether or not to bid.

Health check

It goes without saying to always get an equine vet to thoroughly check over the horse before finally handing over any cash. In America, a pre-purchase veterinary examination tests a horse's overall health and condition. Although this can take time to arrange and be costly, especially if the buyer requests several X-rays or other tests, health problems can be identified before the purchase goes ahead. Whenever possible, the examination should be conducted by an independent vet who is not familiar with the horse and does not work for the seller.

In the UK, the horse's current vet is legally obliged to divulge any problems or injuries he may have treated the animal for previously. Ask the vet to carry out either a 'two stage' (basic) or 'five-stage' (more detailed) vetting, and tell him or her what activities you want to do with the horse.

In the UK, a five-stage vetting, which is carried out on behalf of the purchaser, comprises:

- A preliminary stable examination

- An in-hand examination including trot up, turning and backing

- A ridden exercise period of 20 minutes at all paces, where possible, so that the horse has performed strenuous exercise

- A rest period to allow the horse to settle – the time used to further examine/provide identification documentation

- A final in-hand trot up and foot examination.

Off to a good start

Congratulations! The horse has passed the vet check and you're on the verge of becoming a fully fledged owner! But in your excitement, don't forget to ask the previous owner:

- The date the horse was last wormed, the brand of wormer used and the dosage.

- When the horse was last shod and the name of the farrier – if he's in your area.

- What the horse is currently fed, the quantities, brand names and whether he has any supplements. Is he fed hay or haylage (a dust-free forage cut earlier than hay with a higher water content and nutritional value, that's sealed in plastic – increasingly popular with UK owners, especially those whose horses are allergic to the spores in hay)?

- What's his current routine – when is he fed and how long is he turned out for? Try to replicate this as closely as possible until the horse settles into his new home.

- How much exercise he is used to – and whether that's mainly schooling and/or hacking.

- What tack he currently wears, his bit and blankets/rugs in particular, depending on the time of year.

- Does the horse have any allergies, perhaps to a certain feedstuff or shampoo? Does he headshake and does he suffer from thrush or sweet itch in the summer and mud fever in the winter?

- Finally, does the horse have any idiosyncrasies, quirks or funny habits you should know about – for instance, is he a bit of a Houdini and likes letting himself out of his stable or jumping into the next field, or does he hate having a fly mask put on? Forewarned is forearmed!

Home sweet home

Here are seven ways to introduce your horse to his new surroundings…

1. Walk him round in-hand, so he gets used to his new home without becoming over-excited.

2. Show him other horses at a distance and then let him settle into his stable or stall for a day or so before turning him out. Youngsters and older horses might find being separated from long-time companions a stressful experience.

3. Placing a piece of familiar equipment from his previous home, such as an old blanket/rug or leadrope, into his stable or stall will help reassure and comfort him. Try softly massaging his ears from the base to the tip to help him relax.

4. Turn your horse out in a field on his own at first, so he can see and sniff his future field mates over the fence.

5. Once the other horses have accepted him after a few days, turn him out with them under supervision.

6. Wait a few days before riding your horse so he's had a chance to settle into his new home and routine.

7. The first time you ride your horse at his new home, try to go for a short, relaxing hack in walk so you can both take in your new surroundings and he can get used to the sights and sounds of the immediate area. Also, this puts no pressure on your horse and shows him that there's nothing to be frightened or wary of – heaping further stress on him is the last thing you want to do, especially as some horses take a while to settle into a new barn/yard and routine.

The loan arranger

In many cases, loaning a horse for a set period – say six months – can benefit both the owner and borrower. For instance, the owner may be working abroad or have family commitments, while the borrower may not have the capital to buy a horse or wants a trial period before deciding to splash out permanently.

Get an agreement drawn up including the horse's description (such as any distinguishing marks and brand/tattoo/freezemark/identity chip details); owner's and borrower's names and addresses; where the horse is to be kept; whether he has any allergies or special requirements and the notice period (usually a month but an emergency get-out clause could be included to cover mistreatment).

Detail who is responsible for costs, such as farriery and vet's fees; list any equipment – and its condition – that is also loaned out and state the length of time the agreement is for, who's allowed to ride the horse and what activities can (such as schooling) and can't (such as using the horse for breeding purposes) be undertaken. It is usually down to the lessee to insure the horse at their own expense. Additionally, it's a good idea to include a plan of action if the horse suffers a serious illness or injury and the owner can't be located – can the borrower make the decision to have the horse put down?

You don't need to get a lawyer or solicitor to draw up the document but copies should be dated and signed by both parties. In America, more information about loan agreements can be obtained online from the United States Equestrian Federation, while in the UK, a sample loan agreement can be downloaded from the British Horse Society (BHS) website.

A fair share

If you don't want the responsibility of owning a horse full-time, then sharing, where you contribute towards costs and/or maybe undertake some stable duties, can be the ideal solution. It can benefit the owner, too, as it means the horse is being exercised at times when they perhaps cannot get to the stables. Again, get an agreement drawn up, and before committing, make sure you see the sharer ride your horse in different situations, and that they have the necessary knowledge to groom, tack up and ride your horse without your supervision.

The borrowers

Leasing is less common but involves the horse being lent to another person for a certain period of time in return for payment. Competition or stud horses are sometimes leased.

Honesty is the best policy

Definitely the best advice when selling a horse. If you are truthful about the horse and his abilities, you won't have to refund any money if there are any future disputes, but the buyer can take legal action against you if you fail to disclose a problem you know about.

Don't be tempted to over-inflate the horse's abilities in order to impress potential purchasers – stick to the facts, not your opinion as to what the horse may or may not achieve in the future.

And don't fall into the trap of over-inflating a horse's price either, just because you or someone else believes he has star potential. If you think that the horse could compete at Grand Prix dressage in the future but hasn't yet tackled an unaffiliated preliminary test, prospective purchasers aren't likely to gamble and pay over the odds – especially if the horse's breeding isn't up to scratch. Look at adverts in the 'horses for sale' section of the equestrian press or on the Internet and set the price according to horses of a similar height, age, breeding, breed/type and achievements thus far.

QUICK T!P
TAKING TURNS
If you are leading your horse to show to a vet or potential purchaser, remember to turn him away from you so he doesn't tread on your toes and you don't obscure their view.

Rules is rules

When prospective purchasers test ride your horse, ensure they are wearing the right gear – proper riding boots and a helmet/hat that meet current safety standards – or you could be held negligent if there's an accident.

Also check that they are insured to ride your horse, either through your own cover or theirs.

If someone asks to have your horse for a trial period, insist they are insured and that a written agreement as to who's responsible for what is drawn up first.

It might suit you to sell your horse through a dealer – in which case, make sure you agree to their percentage (usually around 10 per cent) in advance. And check whether you will be liable for any board/livery, farriery or other costs while the horse is between owners. Ask the dealer to sign a document setting out what's been agreed.

Peace of mind

Once you have accepted an offer, draw up a sales agreement, detailing the horse's age, breed, height and past achievements. If the horse has no vices, ask the buyer to sign a statement saying that you have disclosed this to them.

And ask a friend or relative to act as a witness to corroborate your conversation with the buyer.

If the sale subsequently goes sour, don't be bullied into giving the buyer their money back if they say the horse isn't what they wanted after all – that's not a good enough reason!

In the UK, every equine must have a passport that details the animal's age, breed/type, microchip number, medication (so that horses given certain medications, such as phenylbutazone or 'bute' don't enter the human food chain) and appearance, illustrated in a silhouette diagram. It is against the law to buy, sell or move a horse without a valid, up-to-date passport, so don't forget to check that all documentation is fully in order before you sell or buy.

Which breed is best?

There are more than 150 – perhaps as many as 200 – equine breeds in the world today, so deciding which one is right for you can be a real horsey headache. Here are my 10 favorite breeds (in alphabetical order!)…

1. **Andalusian** – this noble breed's agility, balance, action and paces mean it's ideal for High School dressage and as the chosen mount of the Spanish 'rejoneador' (bullfighter). America's best-known feral horse, the Mustang, can trace its roots back to Iberian horses.

2. **Arab** – its powers of endurance and stamina make this showy breed from the Middle East virtually unbeatable at long-distance riding events all over the world. Forward-going, Arabs and part-Arabs are usually agile and can turn their hoof to most equestrian disciplines, although they rarely excel at top-level dressage or showjumping because of their body shape.

3. **Connemara** – Ireland's pony star, the Connemara is courageous, fast, sensible and hardy. The breed excels at showjumping, dressage and showing – especially when crossed with the Thoroughbred. Such are its qualities that 'oversize' Connemaras of 15hh plus are now becoming popular in the UK and Ireland.

4. **Dutch Warmblood** – Holland's leading competition horse has produced some of the world's star equine performers in showjumping, dressage and carriage driving.

5. **Hanoverian** – a German warmblood, the Hanoverian has earned an international reputation as a top-class showjumper and dressage horse.

6. **Irish Draft/Draught** – when crossed with the Thoroughbred to create the Irish Hunter, this athletic former farm horse is a world-beater across country.

7. **Quarter Horse** – arguably America's most versatile breed, the Quarter Horse is the fastest equine in the world over a quarter of a mile. It's popular for rodeos, racing, ranch work and trail riding.

8. **Shetland** – this pint-size pony from the remote Scottish island of the same name is the strongest equine in the world relative to its size. Formerly used down mines and as a pack animal, the Shetland is popular today in harness, as a children's riding pony and as a field companion.

9. **Shire** – this gentle giant from the central English regions or 'shire' counties, weighs between 1800 lbs and 2100 lbs but 2800 lbs isn't uncommon – Mammoth, the largest horse in recorded history, weighed 3300 lbs at his peak. Britain's main source of pre-war industrial and agricultural power, the number of Shires dwindled rapidly during the 20th century but working museums and brewery companies have helped revive the breed.

10. **Thoroughbred** – universally acknowledged as the fastest – and most valuable – breed in the world. Thoroughbreds tend to be sensitive, energetic, intelligent and agile – qualities needed in a good eventer. Not very hardy, though, Thoroughbreds don't tend to winter out well.

A Stable Relationship

❝ *A horse gallops with his lungs, perseveres with his heart, and wins with his character.* **❞**

Tessio

Chapter 2
A Stable Relationship

Horses are herd animals and prefer living outside in their natural surroundings to being in a stable all the time. If your horse is stabled as part of his daily routine, or he is on box rest following an injury, there are various measures you can adopt to tackle boredom and reduce the risk of him developing bad habits.

Boredom breakers

Try to ensure your horse has a clear view of your barn's or yard's activities or he can see, or is close to, an equine pal. Alternatively, swap stables or stalls so that he gets a different view.

It's possible to buy haynets with smaller holes (for haylage) – or placing a haynet inside another haynet will have the same effect – which will take your horse longer to chomp through his daily ration.

Brain teasers

There is a vast array of stable toys on the market, including balls that let out small amounts of food at a time, keeping even the most laid-back of horses occupied for hours. If your horse doesn't show much interest at first, hang up the toy by its handle and smear a small amount of treacle on it.

Alternatively, making your own toy by suspending a turnip or swede on a strand of baler twine from the stable roof or tying a plastic squeezy bottle of peppermint-flavored water to the bars or from the roof, can not only give hours of amusement but encourage mental agility.

Leaving a whole swede on the stable or stall floor for your horse to nibble at is another natural, safe method of 'home entertainment'!

One old tip is to cut bunches of gorse (with gloved hands!) and tie the stalks together, hanging them upside down in his stable. It's said that horses enjoy mouthing the prickly stems.

In addition, to beat boredom, take your horse out for short walks in-hand, perhaps allowing him to graze for 15 minutes, and leave the radio on – rumor has it that horses prefer classical music!

Remember – even turning your horse out in an enclosed area, such as a sand arena or indoor school for half an hour, is better than no turnout at all.

And finally, even chickens and ducks can be good company for a lonely horse!

Door to door

If your horse crib bites while in his stable, deter him by smearing mustard on the top of the door or fit a grille or metal plate/length of tough plastic drainpipe over the stable door.

For horses who scrape the floor in front of their stable door with a forefoot, put a rubber mat there to prevent shoes getting worn and to stop the noise. Similarly, a piece of old carpet or a sack stuffed with straw nailed to the inside of the bottom door will muffle the noise if your horse tends to kick it, especially at feed time.

And if your horse is a barger, fixing a breast bar across the inside of the doorway can remedy this. It's also a good way of keeping the stable cool in summer.

Digging deep

Mucking out is the core duty of any stable management routine. Soiled bedding should be removed from the stable at least twice a day, otherwise leaving a horse standing on it for long periods can lead to him developing breathing and hoof problems – specifically thrush, an unpleasant foot disease.

Which bed is best?

A deep, clean bed keeps a horse warm, encourages him to lie down and soaks up soiling.

Never allow your horse to stand on a bare floor as he will splash his legs when relieving himself, which will discourage him from stalling altogether.

The most popular types of bedding include straw (wheat is best as horses are more likely to eat oat straw), wood shavings (better for horses with an allergy), hemp (highly absorbent; more commonly used in America and Canada), shredded paper and rubber matting (increasing in popularity as owners are recognizing the long-term cost savings).

If your horse has respiratory problems or tends to eat a straw bed, and shavings are too costly, then how about using cardboard or wood fiber/pulp as an alternative? Ideal for owners who prefer to muck out daily rather than skip out a deep litter bed, baled, chopped cardboard is clean, low in dust, highly absorbent and very insulating.

Dried, shredded, wood fiber bedding, on the other hand, provides a warm, comfortable bed and offers low dust levels and excellent absorbency and drainage – perfect if your horse suffers from foot conditions such as thrush. Dried wood pulp can also be deep littered or skipped out daily, plus it's recyclable and 'green'.

QUICK T!P

A CUT ABOVE

No knife or scissors to hand? Then to cut that annoying twine on straw and hay bales, the best solution is, well, another length of baler twine! Use it in a sawing motion to fray the twine you want to remove.

Remember to place all strands of baler twine in a separate bag so they don't get mixed up in bedding or a haynet.

Forking out

When buying a set of barn or yard tools, remember to include a:

- Four-tined fork to muck out straw beds or a shavings fork for, well, shavings

- Broom – brushes with bahia, a natural fibre rather than nylon, are best

- Wheelbarrow

- Shovel

- Pair of rubber gloves to capture those annoying stray droppings

- Knife with a concealed blade for cutting through baler twine and slitting open feed and shavings bags

- Skip or muck basket/plastic laundry basket for skipping out.

Don't muck about!

If your muck heap is becoming more of a mountain than a molehill, then the time has come to reduce this growing blot on your landscape.

Ask your local farmer if he can use the muck as fertilizer on his fields (but not on grazing land due to the risk of worm infestation) in return for taking it away himself. Otherwise an agricultural contractor or removal specialist (look in your local Yellow Pages or the advertising section of the equine press or the Internet) will charge you to remove the muck. Ensure that a tractor has easy access to your muck heap before calling anyone out.

66 *The essential joy of being with horses is that it brings us in contact with the rare elements of grace, beauty, spirit and fire.* **99**

Sharon Ralls Lemon

Muck in!

Keep future muck at a manageable level by advertising it for free to local gardeners via a sign on the road, in your local newspaper/magazine or on the noticeboard at nearby garden centers.

Encourage everyone at the stables to lend a hand to bag up the muck – although some gardeners prefer to collect it straight from the field themselves.

Stable minds

Before building timber stables in the UK, first check whether you need planning permission. You may not need approval if you are replacing existing stables or erecting stables in your garden, but run it by your local council's planning department first. Unless you've built a stable before, it's best to contact specialist contractors for quotes rather than risk a potential DIY disaster!

First foundations

When building stables, 15cm (6in) of hardcore should be put down before laying a concrete base 10cm (4in) deep. A special equine mix of concrete should be used as horse's urine is acidic and can corrode ordinary concrete. The base should slope, enabling urine to drain away, while the stables must have adequate drainage and ventilation. Ideally, they shouldn't face north nor be situated close to trees with far-reaching roots. All stables should have strong timber kickboards extending to at least half the height of the walls.

Getting the brush off

Grooming keeps horses clean and healthy by removing dirt and sweat from their coats, and helps to keep their pores open. It also encourages the blood to circulate and promotes muscle and skin tone, thereby improving the horse's overall condition and appearance.

Also, grooming helps prevent disease and lessens the risk of developing sores and skin problems.

Every well-formed, self-respecting grooming kit should be bursting at the seams with the following items:

- Body brush – to clean the horse's body, mane and tail

- Dandy brush – its stiff bristles are excellent for removing dried mud on legs

- Water brush – for dampening and laying the mane and tail

- Hoofpick – used in a heel-to-toe motion to remove mud and stones from your horse's feet

- Metal, rubber and/or plastic curry comb – the former is solely for cleaning brushes, while the latter two can be used on the horse's body to remove dried mud and loose hairs from the coat

- Sweat scraper – for removing excess water and sweat from the coat following a bath or energetic workout

- At least two sponges – for cleaning the nostrils, eyes and the dock area: baby wipes are good to use on the nose and dock, as they have cleansing and moisturizing properties but don't use them around the eyes or on any broken skin

- Stable rubber, although an old dish towel or tea towel is just as good – for removing dust and giving the coat a final polish

- Mane comb – for combing the mane prior to braiding

- Hoof oil and brush, but pure vegetable oil (or mixing a little high grade pine tar, also known as Stockholm tar, with vegetable cooking oil) can be just as effective – for replacing some of the natural oil in your horse's feet lost in wet, muddy conditions and for adding a finishing touch to your horse's appearance.

Grooming dos and don'ts:

Do:

- Use a rubber curry comb in a circular motion to remove a horse's winter coat as the new summer coat starts to grow through.

- Buy two different colored sponges and delegate which color is to be used for your horse's dock area and which one for the eyes and nostrils – and stick to it.

- Use a small amount of baby oil in water to get rid of dust from your horse's coat, particularly if he's been clipped. Simply wipe over with a wrung out dish towel or tea towel. Baby wipes are great for this too!

- Put a few drops of baby oil on a soft brush and brush through a clean tail to prevent tangles and stop the hair becoming brittle. This helps prevent white hairs becoming discolored, too.

- Hold your horse's tail firmly to one side with your spare hand if he's ticklish and you're grooming round the hindquarters. That way, he's less likely to kick out and you'll feel his tail twitching as an early warning sign if he's cross.

- Clean your grooming kit at the same time as you bathe your horse – otherwise you'll brush dirt straight back into his coat.

Don't:

- Use a dandy brush or plastic curry comb on your horse's mane and tail, as this can cause the hairs to split and break.

- Over-groom a grass-kept horse in winter as this removes the natural grease in his coat, which he needs for protection against the elements. Basic grooming with a dandy brush (not a body brush as its short close-set hairs are designed to really get into a horse's coat to remove dirt and grease) to get rid of dried mud and picking the feet out daily

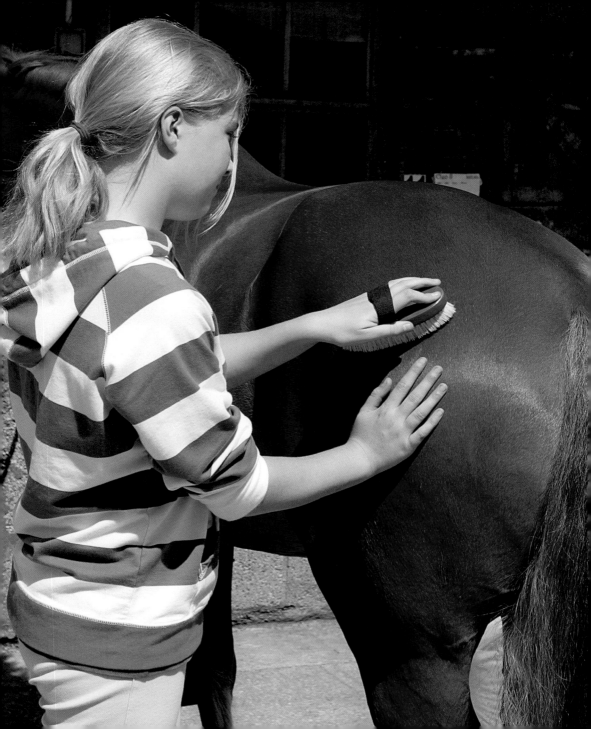

(excrement is full of ammonia, which will attack the hoof if it's not cleaned out regularly) will suffice.

- Clip legs as the hair allows water to drain off the ergot and not into the heel, thereby reducing the risk of winter ailments such as cracked heels and mud fever. Leaving the mane and tail full provides extra warmth.

QUICK T!P

AND REMEMBER...

... if grooming your horse outside his stable, always tie him – using a quick release knot – to breakable string attached to a metal ring. This means that should he pull back, the string, rather than the horse's halter/headcollar or fence post, will break first, and is less likely to cause injury.

A good pick-me-up!

There's nothing more annoying than losing – or someone borrowing and not returning – tools from your grooming kit. Hoofpicks are one of the most likely items to go missing, as everyone needs one and they're so easy to misplace.

How about attaching a length of colorful baler twine to your hoofpick so: (a) It's easier to spot when dropped in your horse's bedding; (b) You can instantly identify it as yours; (c) It can be hung on a nail in the tack room so that you don't have to go scrabbling around for it in the bottom of your grooming box.

Safe not sorry

In today's world, horseowners are no different from any other section of society when it comes to protecting gear, property, transport and even your horse from vandals and thieves. Here are a few ways of stepping up security at your barn or yard…

Be horse smart

Vary the time of day you visit your horse if you can so your movements aren't predicted by a thief.

Have your horse freezemarked, identity chipped/microchipped or your zip code/postcode branded onto his hooves – although the latter method will need repeating as the horn grows downwards. Opportunist thieves are especially less likely to steal a horse with an obvious mark that's easily traced. Plus reputable sales and abattoirs are equipped with scanners to check for identity chips/microchips.

Ideally, turn your horse out without his halter or headcollar – unless he's difficult to catch – to make life harder for would-be thieves.

Do you keep your horse at home? If you have enough land (and no neighbors!), consider installing the best alarm system in the world – a gaggle of geese!

If you live in the UK and your horse is stolen, inform the police and Horsewatch's Stolen Horse Register as soon as possible. Circulate a poster with your horse's photograph and details to local riding schools, tack shops, boarding stables/livery yards, training establishments, studs, feed merchants, vets, sales/auctions and abattoirs.

For horses that are branded, such as having a freezemark, immediately phone the company, which will circulate your animal's details to sales and abattoirs. Also ring your insurance company – they might help you with recovery expenses, depending on the type of cover you have – and call, email and text as many horsey friends as possible to alert them to the fact that thieves are operating in the area.

Guard that gear!

To prevent your gear being stolen or 'permanently borrowed', write your or your horse's name in indelible felt pen on the inside/underside of nylon girths, halters/headcollars and saddle pads/numnahs. Alternatively, sew on name tapes.

Secure your saddle with one of the many different types of saddle lock on the market, while leather and wooden items can be stamped with your zip code/postcode.

Property protection

If budget allows, fit an intruder alarm at the stables and consider installing video surveillance.

Security lights, which come on automatically when they detect movement are a worthwhile investment.

Ensure your tack room door/s are padlocked and have metal bars or a grille fitted to any windows or skylights.

Put up visible notices at the barn/yard and on gates warning that all horses and tack are security marked.

Make sure a padlock and chain are fitted to BOTH ends of gates so that they can't be lifted off their hinges. Alternatively, reverse the top hinge or weld metal plates over the hinges.

Trailers and trucks

Remember to secure your trailer or truck too – both at home and at competitions. Lock all doors and ensure the ramp is up. Try to park it in a well-lit area, as close to other vehicles as possible. Wheel clamps, hitchlocks, lock down devices and installing a GPS tracking device are all excellent ways of deterring thieves.

Mark the vehicle inside and out with your zip code/postcode, including the spare wheel, breast bars and partitions.

Zip/postcoding the roof of the truck or trailer with large letters/numbers in a contrasting color – instantly spotted from the air by any passing police helicopter – is an excellent way to guard against theft as well as recovering the vehicle if it is ever stolen. The wide tape used for silage sacks is ideal for this.

Snap decision

Photograph everything – your horse, tack and trailer/truck – just in case any of your possessions are stolen. Take a hair sample from your horse as this may provide definitive identification, and record any serial numbers on all items of equipment.

Be a nosy neighbor

It makes sense to build good relations with any neighbors, and encourage them to stay vigilant too. Get to know your local Neighborhood Watch coordinator and local police officer – as well as the best way to contact them – and if you live in the UK, find out the name and telephone number of your area Horsewatch coordinator.

Stay alert

Finally, and most importantly, if you see an unfamiliar vehicle parked near your stables or field, note down the licence plate, make of car and time you saw it.

A favorite trick for thieves is to park some distance away and lead a horse back to their trailer or truck. Keep a close eye on trailers or trucks parked in gateways, turnouts, lay-bys or passing places. Be particularly suspicious if you see anyone video recording horses or property as many thieves operate on a 'steal to order' basis.

Check hedges and gates regularly as holes made in the former and bolts and hinges loosened on the latter will often be done in advance to clear exits and hasten departure.

And watch for anything out of the ordinary, such as the barn/yard guard dog sleeping more than usual (he could have been doped).

A Happy Horse

> **" There are fools, damn fools, and those who remount in a steeplechase. "**

Bill Whitbread

Chapter 3
A Happy Horse

Ensuring that your horse is fed a suitable diet, as well as paying close attention to his worming program, teeth and feet, are all part and parcel of responsible horse ownership.

Cut out chopping!

Horses love apples and root vegetables, such as carrots and swedes, as treats or part of their daily diet. When adding these to your horse's feed, ALWAYS slice them lengthways into 'fingers' and NEVER chop them. Otherwise you risk pieces lodging in your horse's throat, causing him to choke.

Oil's well...

Cod liver oil is not only a highly palatable supplement to your horse's diet but it improves bone integrity for healthy joints and helps promote general wellbeing.

Get up and go!

If you feel your horse needs an extra energy boost, perhaps at a show, then give him a banana – minus the skin, of course! The fruit is an excellent source of potassium, needed by nerves and muscles to function effectively.

It's said that a double handful of glucose or a bottle of stout added to a mash or feed can be a good pick-me-up too!

Grub's up!

The 10 golden rules of equine feeding are:

1. Feed little and often – horses have sensitive and relatively small stomachs.

2. Provide a constant supply of clean, fresh water – change regularly as it absorbs ammonia from the stable atmosphere and becomes unpleasant to drink.

3. Feed plenty of good quality hay or haylage, especially in winter when grass has little nutritional value.

4. Add succulents (ie. apples or carrots) to meals to add variety and interest.

5. Feed according to your horse's size, temperament and workload.

6. Introduce any changes to your horse's diet gradually so as not to upset his stomach.

7. Never exercise your horse less than an hour after feeding him.

8. Keep feeding utensils – such as buckets, bowls and scoops – spotlessly clean.

9. Keep food in rat resistent metal or plastic bins with the lids on firmly.

10. Ensure meal times are regular – horses prefer routine.

QUICK T!P

TIRED OUT
Does your horse tend to kick over his bucket at feed time? Then put an end to that trick by placing it inside an old tire.

Fast food!

With horses who bolt their food, try…

… splitting it into three or four small feeds a day;

… putting his feed into a corner manger, which has a larger surface area;

… feed off the floor and spread it around so he can't take large mouthfuls at once;

… Include chaff so he has to chew for longer;

… place a large rounded stone or salt lick/lump of rock salt in the manger so he has to eat around it.

Take care!

Make sure you tie your horse's haynet at the right height – too high and he'll have to stretch up unnaturally for his hay; too low and he might get his feet caught in it.

If you use buckets on the stable floor instead of an automatic water system, it might be safer to remove the handles (and bring the hose to the bucket rather than the other way round!) so your horse can't get caught up or injure himself.

Slowly does it

Is your horse a fussy eater? Encourage him to eat by washing your hands before mixing his feed, as horses can be put off their food by unpleasant smells.

Mix a couple of tablespoons of nutritious and palatable honey into his feed to make it that bit more appetizing. Alternatively, try adding molasses or black treacle (dilute with five parts warm water and sprinkle from a watering can over hay) to sweeten his food. Ensure you are giving sweet-smelling hay. If your horse prefers soaked hay to dry hay, or has an allergy, consider feeding him haylage – which can be sweeter and more palatable. But be sure haylage is from a reputable source and is not moldy.

Ensure the grain or concentrates you buy are fresh by checking the manufacturing rather than 'best before' date (some companies place a three-month shelf life on their feed while others are four months or more). Feed that's past its sell-by date will certainly not go down well with fussy eaters!

Find out what texture of feed your horse prefers – damp, wet, dry, mashed or a combination – and study the ingredients: cubes or mixes? Some alfalfa or grass cubes in low-energy foods can be sour or bitter.

Winter warmers

If your horse starts to lose weight in winter, try adding extra oil – in the form of soya, corn or sunflower oil – to his diet. In the UK, some owners help maintain the weight of older horses with loose or missing teeth by feeding high fiber cubes (or conditioning cubes if there are several missing teeth) as a partial or total hay replacer, soaked into a mash with water or sugar beet pulp.

Sugar beet is commonly fed during winter as it has good energy and fiber levels, is a good succulent, provides liquid in the diet, tempts fussy eaters and can be added to chaff, mixes or cubes to prevent the feed becoming sloppy. But remember to ALWAYS soak sugar beet in cold water for 12 hours (shreds) or 24 hours (pellets) prior to feeding as unsoaked it will swell in the horse's sensitive gut and could prove fatal.

If kept more than 24 hours, particularly in hot weather, sugar beet is also prone to ferment – throw it away if it smells sweet and has turned light brown as it could cause colic otherwise.

Feeding linseed is another way to add both weight and condition – it's easily digestible and can give your horse's coat a healthy bloom. Prepare a jelly by using 20 parts of water to one of linseed and soak for six hours. Strain off the water and replace it with fresh water. Bring it to the boil in a saucepan and simmer uncovered for four hours, stirring occasionally. Feed a teacupful two or three times a week – but check that the seeds have broken first. NEVER feed uncooked linseed as the raw seeds are poisonous.

Breathe easy

If your horse has a respiratory disorder – often exacerbated by dusty stables, indoor schools and the spores in hay and bedding – you may find his condition improves if he's fed good quality haylage, but introduce it gradually so as not to upset his gut. If used within three to five days of opening, haylage has a higher nutritional value and lower dust content than hay, and has a water content of around 35 to 50 per cent, while hay has 15 per cent.

Feeding a garlic supplement, with its expectorant and antibiotic properties, can also benefit horses with mild respiratory problems, such as a runny nose, wheezing or coughing. Garlic also boosts skin condition and the immune system as well as being an effective fly repellent.

Plant power

Provided they are fed under a holistic or homeopathic vet's guidance, herbs can balance deficiencies in your horse's diet. Here are three useful herbs:

1. **Stinging nettle**: Rich in vitamin C, iron, sodium, chlorophyll, protein and dietary fiber, can ward off sweet itch and help circulation – useful for horses with laminitis, rheumatism and arthritis.

2. **Comfrey**: Reputed to heal bone damage, such as sore shins, chipped knees, stress fractures and arthritis, as well as tendon strains. Said to soothe respiratory conditions.

3. **Dandelion**: A good source of potassium, calcium, iron and beta carotene, can aid kidney and liver complaints, stimulate appetite and boost digestion. Useful for rheumatism, arthritis and laminitis.

In good health

A healthy horse will have salmon-pink colored gums, nostrils and third eyelid. Press his gums with your finger – it should take no more than a couple of seconds for the area to return to its normal color.

Get to know what's normal for your horse and become familiar with the shape of his legs so you're more likely to spot any lumps, bumps and swellings as soon as they occur. Check your horse's legs carefully when you bring him in from the field, as this could make the difference between a sound horse and one with a big infected leg that can rapidly develop when a small wound is missed.

Take your horse's respiration, heart rate and temperature regularly (once in summer and again in winter) and record the results so you know what's normal for him…

Too hot to handle?

The normal temperature for an adult horse is 99.5-101.4 °F (37.5-38.5 °C). Foals and yearlings may have a higher temperature, especially if they're nervous.

Take your horse's temperature by greasing the measuring end of a special veterinary thermometer – an easy-to-read digital one is best (although a human glass thermometer will work too, provided you shake the mercury to the bottom of the scale first) – with saliva or petroleum jelly. Insert it 4cm (1.5in) into the horse's anus for one minute, ensuring it tilts against the wall of the rectum. Then remove and wipe the thermometer with cotton wool or a tissue and read it before thoroughly cleaning with cold water and disinfectant. Call the vet if your horse's temperature goes above 102.5 °F (40 °C).

Keep the beat

Find your horse's heartbeat on the left side of his lower chest, just behind the elbow where the girth would go. Remember that a horse's heart rate at rest varies with breed, age and fitness.

It's easier to find your horse's pulse after he has been working, when it is stronger and more obvious. Feel for it on the mandibular artery, under the jaw bone; inside the foreleg just below the elbow; either side of the back of the fetlock or either side of the tail under the dock. Use the flat of your first three fingers and count the number of beats in 15 seconds before multiplying by four to get the pulse rate per minute. The resting heart rate of a healthy adult horse is usually between 26 and 42 beats per minute, but can increase to 200 beats per minute during strenuous exercise. More than 60 beats per minute in an adult horse at rest is definitely abnormal; rates over 80 mean something is REALLY wrong and you should call the vet immediately. Foals, however, have rates of between 70-90 beats per minute.

At competitions, cold water, applied liberally all over your horse – especially to his hindquarters, which produce the most heat – will help bring his pulse down, especially on a hot day.

Take a breather

Your horse's respiration rate at rest should be 8-16 breaths per minute – watch the walls of his abdomen or chest wall move as each breath is taken and count either every inhalation OR exhalation – not both! Respiration rates increase with stress, work or climate changes, while foals have higher respiration rates.

A helping hand

You or your barn/yard should have a first aid kit, stored in a waterproof box, within easy reach in the tack room in case of emergencies. It should include:

- Cotton wool for cleaning wounds but not as a dressing

- A surgical or wound dressing, such as Gamgee (a highly absorbent hospital quality cotton wool pad, encased in a synthetic non-woven cover) popular in the UK, to cushion and protect injuries

- A well-stocked supply of dressings, including Animalintex, an all-purpose veterinary poultice and dressing

- A variety of flexible cohesive bandages to keep dressings in place and provide protection

- Elastoplast to use as an adhesive bandage, particularly for difficult areas like around the knee and hock

- A large animal thermometer for taking your horse's temperature – the digital ones are not only accurate but good if the light is poor

- Blunt ended scissors for trimming hair away from wounds

- Waterproof medical tape for holding bandages or dressings in place

- Wound gel to help combat infection and speed up the healing process

- Salt for making saline solution – NEVER use Dettol on wounds

- A conforming (gauze) bandage

- A cold pack to reduce inflammation and heat

- Tissues

- Antiseptic wash

- Soap

- Exercise/tail bandages

- 50ml syringe

- Petroleum jelly

- Tweezers

- Small flashlight/torch

- Pen and paper

Wound warnings

Horses are always picking up cuts and scrapes in the field or stable, and it's important to treat even the most minor abrasion. Always follow the 'Three C' (clean, clot and cover) rule, whether the injury is a small cut, puncture wound or major laceration:

Wash your hands thoroughly in antiseptic solution before touching any wound. First, gently hose the area with cold water to cleanse the wound, wash away the blood and reveal the wound site. Treat the area – most commonly on the horse's leg – with a wound gel (it might help to trim the hair from the edges afterwards to guard against contamination). Then use a sterile non-adherent dressing to hold the wound gel in place, wrap a layer of cotton wool (or Gamgee in the UK) around the leg followed by a stretch bandage, and secure it in place with a self-adherent bandaging tape such as Vetrap. If a wound is bleeding profusely, try to stop the flow before calling the vet.

Also call the vet if:

- Your horse is lame (even if the wound looks innocent)
- The wound is more than two inches long and has gone right through the skin
- There's a foreign body, such as a stake or piece of metal, embedded in the skin
- If your horse hasn't had an anti-tetanus vaccination
- You suspect a vital structure – such as a joint – may be involved
- The wound is located near or directly over joints or tendons
- A yellowy-colored liquid (joint fluid) is leaking from the wound

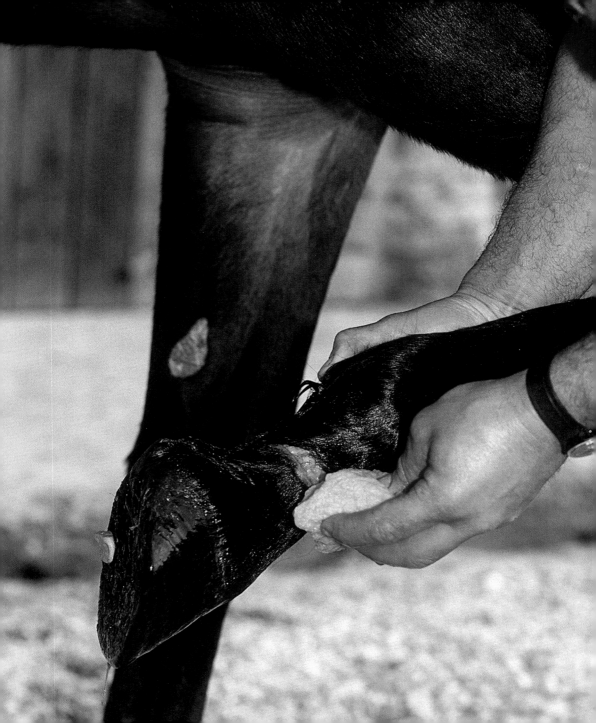

- There is a continuous stream or spurt of blood. Blood from a vein is much darker – maybe even brown – and will ooze rather than gush from a wound as it is flowing back to the heart. A venous injury is less serious than an arterial one, which is much brighter in color, often appearing orange and can spurt as far as seven or eight feet. The average horse has around 50 pints of blood and can lose five pints without it being life-threatening.

In recovery

If your horse tries to take off a bandage with his teeth, use a bib or muzzle or paint the outside of the bandage with a foul-tasting substance.

With a leg injury, bandage the horse's opposite limb as well for support, especially if he's lame and bearing most of his weight on his 'good' leg.

Once a superficial graze has healed over, rub in some petroleum jelly as this will keep the area supple and help prevent the newly healed area from cracking open again.

Remember that wounds heal from side to side, not end to end, so even a big hole that looks like it will never close up, will heal well.

In the UK, the mild astringent and skin cleanser, Witch Hazel – available from all good pharmacies – can be applied externally to any bruised areas and added to water when washing down a horse's legs.

Diapers or nappies make good foot dressings as they are easy to fit, stay on well and are extremely waterproof!

You can disguise the taste of your horse's medicine by using molasses in his feed, hiding it inside an apple, carrot or slice of bread or mixing it with black treacle and smearing it on his tongue with a wooden spoon.

> **" *It's a lot like nuts and bolts… if the rider's nuts, the horse bolts.* "**

Nicholas Evans, The Horse Whisperer

Hot spot

On a hot day, especially if you have been working your horse or competing, watch that he doesn't become dehydrated. Pinch a fold of his skin and if it 'tents' – remains pinched and doesn't spring back to its normal position – then he's dehydrated. Also look for sunken eyes, dry, tacky mucus membranes, and reduced urine output. Offer plenty of water, as well as electrolytes, but don't allow grass or grain/concentrates – hay is OK though.

Some competition horses might benefit from an iron supplement in summer to guard against anemia – but check with your vet first.

Breath of fresh air

If your horse has a dust allergy and coughs (an ailment called RAO – recurrent airway obstruction – formerly known as COPD or chronic obstructive pulmonary disease), there are ways to combat this...

- Feed good quality dust-free hay or haylage or soak your hay for 20 minutes to wash out or swell any mold spores, which will reduce coughing

- Turn your horse out as much as possible so exposure to dust and mold spores in his stable is kept to a minimum

- Ensure his stable has good ventilation

- Muck out while your horse is turned out, to reduce dust levels

- Groom your horse outside

- Store hay and straw as far away from his stable as possible

- Use dust-free or low-dust bedding – rubber matting is the best solution

- For severe cases, a vet might prescribe bronchodilators (for example, Ventipulmin TM, to reverse airway spasm), mucolytics (for example, Sputolosin TM, to help clear mucus from the lungs) or corticosteroids (to reduce airway inflammation).

The latter can be extremely effective but have undesirable side-effects when used in the long-term.

Inhalation therapy – using metered dose inhalers similar to those used by human asthma sufferers – can also help. A plastic 'baby inhaler' spacer is fitted over one nostril while the other is kept closed.

Mud – not so glorious – mud

Mud fever is a common winter ailment, caused by bacteria that affect the heel, pastern and fetlock, resulting in scabs and sores.

With horses – particularly grays and those with white legs – prone to the condition, prevention is better than cure. If yours is susceptible, try to limit his exposure to muddy areas – although this is often easier said than done.

Bring in your horse from the field regularly to allow the mud to dry and be removed. Alternatively, hose the mud off his legs with cold water – warm water will open the pores and encourage bacterial infection to enter the skin – before drying thoroughly and first applying a barrier ointment then breathable bandages or stable bandages over a wound dressing, such as Gamgee in the UK.

Affected horses should have their legs washed daily with a mild antibacterial or homeopathic shampoo and have the scabs removed.

In milder cases, ensure affected areas are clean and dry before applying petroleum jelly and grease to your horse's heels. This will act as a barrier against wet and muddy conditions.

For horses that suffer badly from the condition, try cleaning and drying their legs before applying a good layer of antibacterial cream and then wrapping the affected areas in clingfilm with a wound dressing such as Gamgee (UK) and a stable bandage on top. This causes the legs to sweat, making the scabs softer and easier to remove. But remember to change the dressing once a day.

If the condition becomes serious, stable your horse and ask for veterinary advice, which may include treatment with antibiotics.

Slippery customers

Devising a thorough worming program for your horse ensures his internal organs don't become a parasites' playground!

Change wormers (not just the brand but check the ingredients on the label for a different anthelmintic) every year but not every time so the little devils don't build up a resistance to a certain product, and worm all horses at your barn/yard at the same time. Worm all new arrivals and keep them stabled for 48 hours afterwards so that they don't contaminate the pasture.

In December, give your horse a single dose of ivermectin (a broad-spectrum anti-parasitic avermectin medicine) to cut short the cycle of the botfly, which lays its characteristic yellow eggs on horses' legs in the summer.

Place worm powders in the fridge a day or so before giving to your horse as this helps reduce the smell and makes them more palatable.

Feet first

The phrase 'no foot, no horse' has never been more true. Horses need new shoes every six to eight weeks – or even less if you ride a lot on the roads. But even if your horse is unshod, he should still have his feet trimmed regularly by a qualified farrier.

If you find your horse is suffering from crumbling or splitting hooves and can't keep metal shoes on, try putting an egg in his feed every day – you

should find the new growth is far stronger thanks to the extra protein. Alternatively, for a similar effect, rub in mutton fat from the Sunday roast or local butcher shop/meat market or add a sachet of gelatine dissolved in a mugful of hot water to a feed each day.

Does your horse tend to trip or stumble – perhaps because he's getting on in years? Then ask your farrier about fitting rolled toes on the front shoes, and possibly the hind ones too. This will enable your horse to roll his foot off the ground rather than having to lift it uncomfortably high.

For riders who are restricted to hacking mainly on the roads, and find their horses tend to slip on the surface, ask your farrier to fit a road nail (a stud with tungsten pin inserts), or a pair of road studs if extra grip is needed, into each shoe.

Teeth trouble

If your horse eats very carefully or takes longer than normal to eat; there's a lot of undigested food in his droppings; he 'quids' (drops food out of his mouth) or there's any strong/unpleasant smell from his mouth, then it's time to call an equine dentist.

Don't ride your horse – or use a hackamore (bitless bridle) until the dentist has been – it could just be his teeth need rasping to file down any sharp edges.

It makes sense for your horse to have a yearly dental check-up as painful teeth may explain various riding and/or behavioral problems.

A splashing time

For those of us lucky enough to live near the sea or a safe-flowing river – or even an equine swimming pool – it's worth taking the plunge and introducing your horse to water therapy for the following reasons…

- To vary routine – swimming is excellent for sweetening up bored or sour horses, particularly those on box rest following an injury

- Following certain operations, particularly knee or fetlock arthroscopies

- For laminitics, because swimming keeps the weight off their feet

- For horses with tendon and ligament strains and foot problems such as bruised feet

- To help reduce general bruising, stiffness and soreness

- For horses with bad backs

- As part of your exercise or fittening routine, particularly if the ground is too wet in winter or too hard during the summer or due to frost. Endurance horses, trotters, hunters, racehorses, point-to-pointers, eventers, showjumpers, show ponies and police horses have all benefited from horsey hydrotherapy.

An easy catch

So you can't catch your horse? A common problem, this one. Nothing is more annoying than being unable to get your horse in from the field, especially when the weather is foul or you're in a hurry.

In a herd situation, horses develop certain roles like lookouts, followers and leaders. Establish which horse yours prefers to follow, and bring him in first. Often, once all the other horses have been caught, even the most wilful may decide it's best to come in after all.

Alternatively, walking confidently up to a horse's shoulder so he can see you coming clearly, and making slow, deliberate movements so as not to startle him, can make all the difference.

Other tricks like rustling a crisp packet, hiding the halter/headcollar and rattling some feed or stones in a bucket may sometimes help, too.

QUICK T!P
TURNING THE TABLES
When turning your horse out, don't allow him to gallop off into the distance, spraying you with dirt and mud. Instead, turn him calmly to face the gate before taking off his halter/headcollar. That way you're less likely to get kicked.

Having a field day

Patrol pasture on a regular basis to ensure it remains a safe haven for your horse. As well as keeping the level of droppings to a minimum, pick up any rubbish, fill in rabbit holes/tramp down molehills, mend broken fencing, remove protruding nails and pull up and burn any poisonous plants (see pages 72 & 73). Nail broken rails on to your horse's side of the post – this will make it more difficult for him to push them off in the future by leaning or rubbing against the fence.

Watch out for anyone throwing yard waste or grass cuttings into your horse's field – remove immediately as this can cause colic if eaten.

When feeding hay in the field, always put out one pile more than the number of horses to prevent squabbling.

Land laws

Don't overstock your land – aim for a minimum of one acre per horse, and for better and easier pasture management, use electric fencing to split larger fields into smaller areas that can be alternately grazed and then rested.

Rotate paddocks so each one is rested for three to four weeks, in order to give grass the chance to recover.

New beginnings

Harrowing your pasture between late March and April in the UK, Europe and America, when the ground starts to dry up will not only help level the rough potholed areas but is an excellent way to spread grass seed, stimulate grass growth, remove moss and weeds and spread droppings.

If the field is too large to remove droppings by hand, harrowing and resting the field will help reduce the risk of worm infestation. However, avoid harrowing wet areas as this will leave unsightly wheel-track marks and may stunt grass growth.

Rolling the field a couple of days later will level the uneven surface and pack down loose soil. It will also encourage any newly laid grass seed to germinate.

Getting to the grassroots

Consider grazing your horse with sheep in winter – these 'lawnmowers' are good for 'patting' down softer land without causing damage but don't allow them to pull up the roots – and cattle, which like the longer grass that horses reject, in summer. If done properly, this can help improve your pasture and lower the worm burden.

No access

Here are 10 poisonous plants to protect your horse from…

1. **Privet** – luckily this shrub is rarely serious unless eaten in large quantities. The toxin glycoside ligustrin can cause diarrhea and colic. Watch out for privet hedges bordering pasture or people dumping their yard/garden cuttings.

2. **Bracken fern** – the leaves and root of this plant contain thiaminase and are poisonous green or dried. Later symptoms include depression and rear leg weakness, coma and eventual death.

3. **Acorn/oak leaves** – new leaves and green acorns are the most toxic as they contain higher levels of tannins (weak acids). If a horse eats large quantities, severe gastrointestinal, kidney and liver damage can occur, followed by death. Use electric fencing around oak trees if the leaves are within reach or during the autumn and remember to pick up acorns blown into the field.

4. **Potato** – research has shown that horses are more susceptible to potato poisoning than ruminants, even when non-green potatoes have been fed. Green parts of the plant are the most toxic, especially the skin of greened tubers.

5. **Tansy ragwort/common ragwort and groundsel** – the alkaloids in these bright yellow daisy-like weeds cause staggering, loss of appetite and condition, straining to pass dung and gradual liver damage, usually fatal within a month. Small amounts eaten over a long period of time will have the same effect as one large dose, while the plant is more toxic and palatable in hay. In the UK, ragwort is classified as an injurious weed under the 1959 Weeds Act and landowners can be forced to remove it.

6. **Common or European yew** – this evergreen shrub or small tree native to Europe is lethal even when eaten in small quantities – a horse ingesting just 0.05 per cent of its bodyweight will die within five minutes.

7. **Foxglove** – this herb with its characteristic pinkish-purple, white, yellow or orange tubular flowers is mostly associated with the English countryside but can be found in parts of Europe and North America, and contains cardiac glycosides (including digitoxin and digoxin). Horses often die within 8-12 hours of consuming a lethal dose – usually in hay, although animals that have only ingested a small amount may recover in a few days following treatment.

8. **Belladonna/deadly nightshade** – death from cardiac arrest can occur when large quantities of this perennial herbaceous plant are consumed. Native to Europe, North Africa and Western Asia, but naturalized in parts of the US, it is a member of the same family as tomato and potato.

9. **Water hemlock** – with its fern-like coarsely-toothed leaves and clusters of small white flowers in an umbrella shape, this plant is easily confused with celery, wild parsnips, parsley and carrots – but smells of mice. It's common in North America (considered to be the most violently toxic plant here) and Europe – only a small amount ingested can result in convulsions and death.

10. **Locoweed** – two main variations commonly grow across North, Central and South America and one in Australia. Grazing of this plant, which has flowers resembling sweetpeas, causes chronic intoxication, depression, emaciation and incoordination. Horses may recover from poisoning but brain deterioration can make them dangerous to ride.

BORDER CONTROL

Ensure the fencing around your horse's field is no higher than his back – to discourage him from jumping out. Aim for a height of between 1m 7cm (3ft 6ins) and 1m 37cm (4ft 6ins). The gap between the lowest rail and the ground should be a maximum of 46cm (1ft 6in) – otherwise a horse might try to get underneath.

Bright idea

Temporary electric fencing is versatile, easy to use and ideal for strip-grazing and sectioning off areas of land. However, it should be checked every day, as it can become loose in wet and windy weather.

Introduce horses to electric fencing gradually – it's best to erect it near a permanent fence at first before moving it further in.

Make electric and wire fencing more visible by tying strips of colored plastic to it at regular intervals.

When running an electric fence, use a leisure battery (designed for travel trailers/caravans or boats, which don't need a constant charge) as opposed to a car battery (designed to be charged constantly by the car's generator). This will maintain a charge for longer, plus the battery will have a longer life.

Keep batteries well ventilated, clear of naked flames and prevent sparks by disconnecting the charger from the mains power supply before removing the clips from the battery. Don't touch battery connections at the same time!

A close shave

If you plan to work your horse regularly in winter, his thick protective coat will need to be clipped so that he doesn't sweat too heavily, become uncomfortable and lose condition.

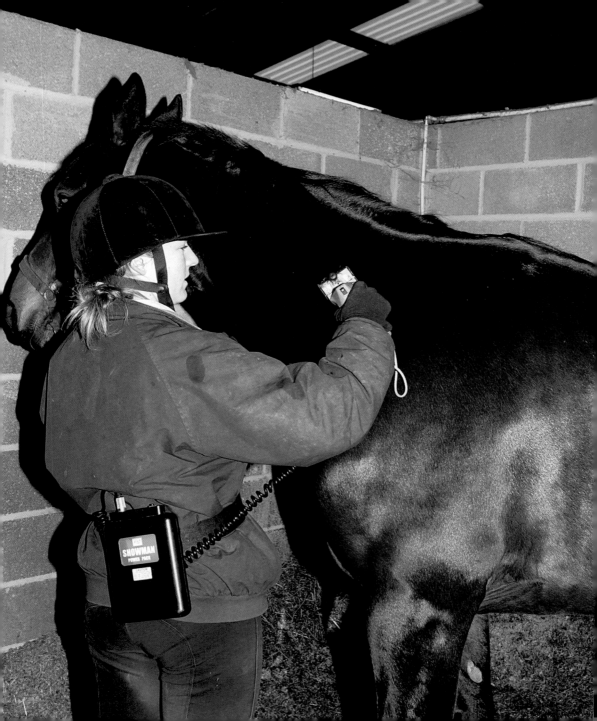

The more frequently your horse is ridden, the more hair should be removed – if he's just worked at weekends, a belly, strip or bib clip (see below) should suffice, while horses that are in full work and mainly stabled would probably require a hunter clip.

Choose from the following types of clip…

- Belly/strip/bib – when the minimal amount of hair is removed, which is ideal for horses in light work; hair from just the lower part of the neck and under the belly is removed

- Trace – suits horses that are worked several times a week; hair from the lower part of the neck and sides is clipped, which can vary from a low to high trace clip. Popular for eventers.

- Irish/chaser – a variation of the above whereby hair is removed from a line below the poll to the stifle, with hair left on the legs. A popular clip for steeplechasers as it keeps horses' backs warm but also allows for hard work.

- Blanket – good for horses who are ridden every day; just the hair on the back and quarters is left

- Hunter – virtually a full clip, with just hair on the legs and saddle area remaining

- Full body clip, body clip or full clip – the most popular clip in many equestrian disciplines in the US; all hair is removed, including from the face and legs.

" *I have a new horse. I get her to come to me from half a mile away. With just a simple call. That's because she knows that when she's with me, she's taken care of. She trusts me.* **"**

Russell Crowe

It's a snip!

If your horse is prone to being a bit fresh and putting in the odd buck, consider giving him a blanket clip – thereby keeping the hair on his hindquarters – rather than a hunter or full clip.

Short-necked horses will gain a more swan-like appearance with a blanket clip sited further back than normal.

First things first

Before clipping, ensure your horse's coat is clean and well-brushed as matted hair will blunt the clipper blades more quickly. Check your clipper blades are sharp – blunt ones can leave lines or steps. Sharpened blades are better than new blades – ensure you have two pairs in the same condition or you'll end up with a two-tone horse!

Bandage or braid/plait your horse's tail to ensure stray hairs don't get caught in the blades when you're clipping around his flanks.

Make your mark

For a slinky, even clip, it's best to mark lines on your horse's coat BEFORE switching on the clippers! Damp chalk is good for this, although it can rub off and can't be seen on grays, while many people prefer using home decorating masking tape. But make sure your horse stands squarely on a flat surface.

Ensure the lines are equal on both sides by using a piece of baler twine as a template across your horse's withers.

Smooth operator

Use a light pressure with long strokes to avoid the coat appearing stripy.

Always clip in the opposite direction to the hair where it changes direction, such as under the gullet, on the stifle and around whorls.

Clip tips for equine first-timers

If your horse has never been clipped before, or is nervous of the clippers, run them over the back of your hand first so he gets used to the noise and vibration.

Acclimatize him further by taking the clippers into his stable every day – switched on – without attempting to clip him. If this freaks him out, go back a step and just go in with the clippers switched off and run them over his coat so he gets used to how they feel.

Plugging your horse's ears with cotton wool or sewing sheepskin into the ears of a fly fringe will help to muffle the sound, while clipping in the stable may help too (remember to put a small amount of bedding down and throw it away afterwards as it will be full of hair and clipper oil). Alternatively, opt for a pair of low-vibration or battery-operated clippers or ones that have a variable speed.

Gradually build up clipping a nervous horse – just do the neck in two strokes to begin with. Move on to the shoulder and leave difficult or sensitive areas – such as the head – until last when hopefully the horse will have become more accustomed to the experience.

Tie him up with calm horses and clip them first so he gets used to the noise and learns there's nothing to be worried about.

Under control

A humane twitch can be used with expert help if a horse is difficult or unpredictable, or sedation – under a vet's guidance – as a last resort.

When clipping ticklish or sensitive areas, such as the belly or around the genitals, ask an assistant to distract the horse with a carrot, pinch a fold of skin on his neck to relax him or lift a foreleg to prevent him from kicking out.

It's best to leave hair on your horse's legs for protection. Follow the lines of the muscles and aim for an inverted V at the top of the foreleg while the clip should slope up towards the stifle on the hindleg. If your horse objects to a foreleg being clipped, ask a helper to pick up and hold the opposite foreleg. With a hindleg, the foreleg on the same side that's being clipped should be picked up and held. Clip an inverted V at the top of the tail, too.

Safe and sound

Always use a circuit breaker if opting for electrically-operated clippers.

Remember to wear rubber soled footwear and tie your hair back if it's long!

When clipping a difficult horse or there's a chance the horse will kick, form a chest-high barrier between you by using a couple of bales of hay, straw or shavings stacked on top of each other. This will limit the range of movement and absorb any impact if the horse does kick out.

When to clip

In the UK and America, from September/October – depending on the weather – is usually a good time if your horse has not been clipped during the summer. Some horses are clipped all year round if they are competing. Often, older horses are also clipped in the summer as some do not fully lose their winter coat.

If you only clip your horse during winter, you should do the last clip of the year no later than the first couple of weeks in January when your horse will soon start to grow his new summer coat.

As snug as a bug!

When your clipped horse isn't being worked, remember to use a quilted blanket/rug in the stable and a waterproof blanket/rug outdoors, to compensate for the loss of his natural coat.

Check your horse's blanket/rug fits him snugly by ensuring that:

- The top lies 5-10.2cm (2-4ins) in front of the withers;

- It finishes just as the tail starts (unless it has a tail flap);

- The outside edge is well in front of the shoulder to allow for free movement;

- You can fit two hands' width between his chest and the front straps;

- The top front strap is in line with the point of the shoulder;

- You can't see your horse's belly when the blanket/rug is done up.

If outdoor blanket/rug straps are clean, supple and correctly-fitting but still tend to chafe, try slipping a length of bicycle inner tube over them.

Saddle up!

" The wind of heaven is that which blows between a horse's ears. "

Arabian proverb

Chapter 4
Saddle up!

Choosing the right tack and keeping it in good condition is vital, ensuring both you and your horse are comfortable while you're in the saddle.

There are different types of English style saddle to suit various activities (ie. general purpose for all-round riding activities as well as specialist showjumping, dressage and side saddles) plus hundreds of bits (from a simple jointed snaffle to a Dutch gag, for controlling strong horses across country more easily).

New saddles should be fitted by a qualified saddler and re-checked, ideally twice a year, while choosing a bit is best left in the hands of a knowledgable person.

Saddle checks

It's important your horse's saddle fits him correctly. A badly-fitting saddle can cause discomfort and lead to behavioral problems. Watch out for:

- Uneven stirrup bars that aren't in a neutral position, are inset deeply or are pointing inwards towards the horse

- A gullet that's less than 7.6cm (3ins) wide all the way along

- Any lumps, bumps or sharp points each side of the gullet, under the panels

- Girth straps attached at an unequal distance from the knee rolls on both sides

- A saddle that's too long – there should be at least 15cm (6ins) between the horse's loins (measure from the change in hair pattern at the horse's hips) and the rear of the saddle.

- A tree that's too wide (where the saddle sits too low and places pressure on the withers and spine) or too narrow (so it pinches the withers and spine). When the saddle has been correctly placed on the horse but not girthed up, you should be able to fit three fingers between the horse's withers and the pommel, and the flat of your hand between the front of the tree and the horse's shoulder, immediately behind his scapula, and slide your hand evenly from top to bottom. Tightness at the top or bottom indicates that the angle of the tree and angle of the horse's shoulder are not compatible. For horses with high withers, a saddle with a cut back pommel may give a better fit.

If your horse has been out of work for some time, harden up the skin around his girth and saddle area by applying rubbing alcohol (surgical spirit in the UK) or salt water to reduce the risk of sores or galls.

Girth reminders

For a girth to fit correctly, ensure that there are at least two spare holes either side on the girth straps to allow for stretching leather.

After tightening the girth and before mounting, pull each foreleg forwards to iron out any wrinkled skin behind the elbow.

Slip the girth into a sheepskin sleeve if it is chafing your horse, more likely with youngsters or horses who are unfit or being brought back into work.

To wash non-leather girths (check the label first!), pop them in an old pillowcase in the clothes washer/washing machine, so the buckles don't damage the drum.

Bits 'n pieces

Ensure your horse's bridle fits correctly by slotting two fingers underneath the noseband (unless it's a crank-style noseband), a fist underneath the throatlatch and two fingers underneath the cheekpieces.

Check your bit is the perfect fit for your horse's mouth by measuring 1cm (0.4in) between the cheekpiece (or ring) and the mouth. The bit should be high enough in the mouth to gently crinkle the corners – if it's too low it will bang against your horse's teeth.

When looking for a new bit, use a saddler that runs a 'bit library' so you can try before you buy.

Sometimes a young horse can benefit from a smear of petroleum jelly on the outside of the corners of his mouth before the bit is put in, just to keep his skin supple and comfortable while he learns to take the bit.

Don't confuse the French link bit, which has a kidney-shaped central plate, with a Dr Bristol, which has a flat-sided one. The former minimizes pressure and is a mild bit, while the latter applies pressure and is more severe.

Bitguards are rubber discs that are good for keeping a snaffle bit central in the horse's mouth but can be tricky to fit. Soak them in hot water first – to make them more malleable – and thread two pieces of baler twine through the disc. Ask a friend or use a tack cleaning hook or door handle to help you stretch it enough to fit the ring of the bit through.

If you want to start riding in a double bridle for the show ring or a dressage test, practice first by attaching two pairs of reins to a snaffle until you become more confident and dexterous.

With stirrup irons, they should be 2.5cm (1in) wider than the broadest part of your foot, to ensure your feet don't get stuck.

Mentioning martingales...

If your horse wears a standing martingale (also known as a head check, which runs from the girth via the neck strap to the noseband) – which helps prevent him raising his head too high and beyond the point of control – check it's not fitted too tightly by pushing it up into his gullet. If it doesn't reach, it's too tight and will restrict his movement.

For more consistent control across country or when jumping, you could try adding an extra rubber stop to each rein to limit the movement of a running martingale (sometimes known as 'rings').

The running martingale – a strap which runs from the girth to the neckstrap or breastplate where it splits off to each rein – encourages the horse to lower his head by placing pressure on the bars of his mouth via the reins. It provides greater freedom than the standing martingale.

A Market Harborough (also called the German martingale) is used mainly as a training aid, acting in a similar manner to the running martingale but with greater leverage.

The Irish martingale (sometimes known as a semi-martingale) – most commonly seen on European racehorses – is not a martingale in the truest sense. It is simply a strap that connects both reins, keeping them from coming over the horse's head and getting entangled in the event of a fall.

QUICK T!P
BOOTED UP!
To make it easier to pull on rubber bell or overreach boots, soak them in hot water first. Smear a little petroleum jelly around the tops so they slide freely around the pastern without chafing the skin.

Prevent your horse from getting boot rubs – and stop the boots from slipping – by fitting an elastic cotton bandage (such as a Tubigrip) underneath.

Powder power

Sprinkle a little talcum powder on a natural sheepskin saddle pad/numnah before gently brushing it out to absorb sweat and dirt and help keep it clean.

Clean and sparkling

Tack must be cleaned regularly to keep it in tiptop condition and to ensure dirt and grease don't irritate your horse. When cleaning saddlery, follow the grain of the leather, as this will help retain its strength.

Save up all your ground down bits of saddle soap and heat in an old saucepan, together with some milk. Leave to cool before applying it to your leather tack to create a great shine.

Disguise any marks on your saddle by dampening them and rubbing with the back of a spoon in the direction of the grain. Also, gentle circular rubbing with a knot of horse hair will help reduce lines and marks caused by buckles.

To remove dirt from small and difficult areas of your tack, such as stirrup treads and the corners of your horse's bit, use an electric toothbrush (with a spare head, of course!).

Clean curb chains and bit rings – but not the mouthpiece – with metal polish, rinse and put them in your jeans pocket. The rubbing of your legs will soon shine them up!

If you've just bought new tack, wrap it in newspaper overnight when it has been oiled, to darken the leather and stop the oil evaporating.

When buying secondhand gear, ensure you clean it with an anti-bacterial wash before using it. Always disinfect moldy tack as normal cleaning will not destroy the fungal spores, which can cause skin infections.

And if the worst comes to the worst, you can always breathe life into dry and brittle leather that has been overexposed to the sun or heat by applying warm oil. Apply a second coat a few days later when the first has soaked in.

Weather woes

If it starts to rain heavily while you're riding, resist the temptation to dry your saddle and bridle quickly with a hair drier or by using direct heat from a radiator. Leather that dries too quickly becomes cracked and brittle. Instead, wash off mud and dirt with warm water – never use hot water as leather will scald, just like our skin would. Then let your tack dry naturally in a room that's not damp or cold nor has the central heating on full blast. When most of the excess moisture has dried but the leather is still slightly damp, rub in some glycerine saddle soap. Once dry, use some oil or hide food sparingly.

In storage

Storing tack over the winter and want it to stay in tiptop condition until the spring? Then bear the following three points in mind…

1. Don't allow your leather to dry out, otherwise it will peel and crack. Use a leather food to prevent this from happening.

2. Store your tack at room temperature in dry conditions – leather stored in a damp or humid atmosphere is more likely to become moldy. Attics or wine cellars – less likely to suffer extremes of temperature – are good places.

3. It's a good idea to wrap leather items in a cotton sheet, pillowcase or towels as cotton will absorb any moisture in the atmosphere before the leather can. Don't use polythene as any dampness will not be able to escape, which could encourage the leather to become moldy. Some professional grooms cover leather tack in petroleum jelly before wrapping it in a linen sheet, to protect it from mold and discoloration during long-term storage.

All aboard!

If you're learning to ride, or returning to the saddle after a break, it's a good idea to book a series of lessons with a qualified riding instructor to get you off on the right foot and build confidence. In fact, even good riders benefit from the odd lesson occasionally.

Remember that there are four 'natural' aids in English riding: the hands, seat, legs and voice, while 'artificial' aids include spurs, bits/hackamores and whips/crops or 'bats'.

On your marks...

If riding English style, first tighten the girth and run the stirrup irons down their leathers. Ask a helper to hold the horse's head and the off side (right) stirrup leather, to prevent the saddle from slipping while you mount up.

Now, stand on the near (left) side of the horse, gather the reins and hold the pommel with your left hand. Face the horse's tail and turn the iron clockwise with your right hand. Place your left foot in the iron and grip the waist of the saddle with your right hand. Spring off the ground and straighten your left leg as you swing your right leg over the horse's back, taking care to clear the cantle of the saddle. Remember to move your right hand forward. Gently lower yourself into the saddle, gather your reins and turn the right iron clockwise before placing your foot in it.

QUICK T!P
GOING UP...?
Riders who are not very mobile or are nervous should ask their instructor if they can climb aboard using a mounting block. Not only is this good for bad backs and stiff legs but it puts less strain on the saddle.

When mounting from the ground, don't put too much of your foot in the iron as your toe will dig your horse in the ribs.

The long and short of it

If you're not sure whether your stirrups are the correct length, there are four simple ways to check:

1. Stand facing your horse's side and lift the flap of the saddle. Place your right index finger on the stirrup bar and, with your left hand, run the stirrup leather along the length of your outstretched arm. The bottom of the stirrup iron should just reach your armpit.

2. If the near side stirrup is higher than the top of your legs, you'll be putting excess strain on the saddle, your horse's spine and your joints when you mount. Solution: stand on higher ground or a mounting block, let the stirrup down a few holes or find a horse with shorter legs!

3. Once on board, let your legs dangle freely down your horse's sides. The bottom of the stirrup iron should reach your ankle bone.

4. Position your legs correctly without the stirrups – if you have to drop your toes to reach the irons then your leathers are too long.

Remember to swap your stirrup leathers around as, over time, the near side one will stretch if you mount from the ground, and your feet will be uneven in the irons.

Position pointers

When working on your posture in the saddle, think about recreating a standing up position while on board. There should be a vertical line from your shoulder, through your hip to your heel. Sit straight with your shoulders and hips square to your horse's shoulders. Reviewing your position with mirrors, your instructor or a friend using a camcorder or video camera will help you identify any bad habits.

Sit taller in the saddle by looking up and ahead. This will encourage your horse to look up, freeing his shoulder so his hind legs can come through and carry his weight better.

Visualization can work wonders when you're on board. Imagine you are riding a tube of toothpaste, and you are trying to squeeze toothpaste from the back out through the nose.

Try some suppling exercises before climbing aboard: stretch your legs; lean backwards, forwards and to the sides; roll your head, neck and shoulders and swing your arms. Your posture will be better, you'll feel more relaxed and your horse will pick up on that. Allow your horse to stretch before working him too!

It may be a tough wake up call for your rear end but working your horse for short periods without stirrups will help strengthen your position in the saddle, improve your balance and make you a more effective rider – honest!

A good exercise to help strengthen your leg position when you're not riding is to place the balls of your feet on the edge of a step, about two feet apart. Stay upright in your back and allow your heel joint to relax and drop. Bend your knees a little, then work on stretching the back of your legs and keeping your balance. Or try walking slightly pigeon toed!

Hand signals

To obtain a light contact with the horse's mouth, your hands must remain still but flexible and follow the horse's movement. There must be a straight line from the horse's mouth to the rider's elbow. Hold your hands vertically with the thumbs on top, slightly above and just in front of the withers. Imagine you are carrying a tray with cups of tea, or that you are holding the bit in the horse's mouth without a bridle, using only the reins for control.

If you find you are constantly having to shorten your reins when you ride – perhaps because the horse is being lazy and not working from behind so is more heavier on the hand – wind a rubber band around each rein as a marker for where your hands should normally be. A simple and discreet tip!

Att-en-tion!

Getting your horse to halt squarely is an important part of performing a successful dressage test. If you find that one hind leg is further back, place your leg behind the girth on that side and nudge him forward. If it's a front leg that's at fault, nudging in front of the girth with your lower leg can remedy this. Always adjust the halt forwards, not backwards.

QUICK T!P
TROTTING ON
Steady trotting up hills and inclines is a great way of maintaining your horse's fitness levels.

Coordinating canter

Don't allow the reins to become slack when asking for canter as this will result in your horse running forwards in trot instead. Ask for a canter while sitting up because tipping forwards will unbalance your horse and make it difficult for you to maintain the pace.

Cantering on a 'straight' circle, asking for an inside bend, will encourage your horse to take his weight on to his inside hind leg and create a more balanced pace.

Ask your horse to leg yield in canter from the track – this is a useful exercise to encourage him to work from the outside.

Ready for take off?

Do you have problems seeing a stride when jumping? Then a good exercise is to put a placing pole one of your horse's canter strides in front of the fence.

If you're in the habit of seeing a long stride and encouraging your horse to stand off his fences, try looking at the base of the fence rather than the top rail as you approach. Let the fence come to you, and it should help draw you closer into the fence.

For horses that rush their fences, go back to basics. Work your horse in trot around – but not over – poles on the ground, through wings and around markers, using lots of turns, circles and changes of direction. Then introduce one pole and trot over it, followed by three poles, before progressing to a small crosspole and finally an upright of the same height. Ask your horse to return to walk after each jump. This exercise should help temper both over-enthusiasm and greenness in a young horse.

Making strides

Schooling exercises are great for boosting balance, suppleness and accuracy – for you and your horse!

If you feel your horse tends to run on and get away from you, ride small circles to rebalance him.

Why not try schooling your horse one meter in from the outside track? You'll really have to concentrate but it's a great test of your outside rein and leg awareness and should improve straightness and security of the outline. Aim for straightness out of the corners and don't allow your horse to drift towards the fence or kicking boards.

A good suppling exercise is to ride three or four serpentine loops with a complete circle in the end of each loop before moving on to the next one.

When riding circles, maintain a consistent contact by resting your outside hand on the horse's withers, opening the inside rein so your hand is above the horse's shoulder and rotating your upper body to help turn the horse.

If your circles tend to be more egg-shaped than round and your lines more wavy than straight, how about using flour and a tape measure to mark out an accurate circle or straight line in the arena? Instead of drawing the whole circle, use dots instead.

Does your horse tilt his head while you're schooling him? Then try raising your inside hand for a brief moment, before returning it to the correct position. The more a horse leans, the lower your hands should be.

If you find you are pulling against a forward-going horse, give with the inside rein to discourage him from fighting the contact.

Back to school

Once in a while, ask your instructor to ride your horse to refresh him, and also for you to see how your instructor asks for certain movements and how your horse responds from the ground. Ask friends and family to watch you ride, too. Even a non-rider can often spot if parts of you looks stiff or a little out of balance – sometimes they can notice a real improvement! Alternatively, ask them to video you so you can judge what you need to work on to execute that perfect turn or transition for yourself.

If you're schooling your horse after a hectic day, and you're getting more and more wound up, take a deep breath and smile! Smiling helps to relax your mind and body.

Whatever your level, and whether you compete or ride for pleasure, learning from others can be really inspiring. So go along to a show or event, or even hire an instructional DVD, to soak up some of the professionals' approaches and techniques – you're bound to be able to apply one or two!

Be prepared

You can never be too careful when going for a ride or hack. Always let someone know your route before setting off alone. Ensure the following items are packed in a bumbag around your waist or in small backpack before setting off on a long ride:

- A fully charged cell/mobile phone (or some coins to make a call from a phone kiosk/box in an emergency). Ensure you have stored the numbers of your barn/yard and vet in your phone.

- Strand of baler twine (in case you need to tie up your horse)

- Card with the name and number of who to contact in an emergency, plus details of any allergies, in case you are found unconscious by the emergency services

- Hoofpick (to extract stones from your horse's feet)

- Leadrope

- Small basic equine and human first aid kits (if there's room)

- Map, route and compass

- Insect repellent (human and equine) and sunscreen – if the weather's warm

- Whistle, for attracting attention

- Bottles of water

Time to reflect

If riding on the roads, both you and your horse should wear high visibility clothing, whatever the weather as a bright sunny day can affect a driver's vision just as much as bad light. Some riders believe pink, as opposed to yellow or orange, is a more obvious color. Wearing a tabard with the words 'slow down for horses' or 'caution young horse' helps too.

If you can't avoid riding on the roads when the light fades, fit a safety lamp (white to the front, red to the rear) to the stirrup nearest the traffic.

In advance

As well as putting your horse's halter/headcollar on under his bridle, it's a good idea to attach an identity tag with a contact telephone number onto your horse's saddle – just in case you part company when you're out riding.

Check your horse's shoes for looseness, and tune in to the weather reports before you leave – never set out if storms or thunder and lightning are forecast. Protect yourself and your horse against insects and sun in the summer.

If your horse isn't keen to leave the barn/yard, ride forward positively and firmly, ideally with another rider on a schoolmaster (an older, more experienced horse) to give him security and confidence. Ask your horse to take the lead for short distances. Re-enforce your leg aids with your whip, then praise him and relax when he obeys. Using your voice will work wonders in encouraging and calming a nervous horse.

En route

In the UK, always observe the Countryside Code and shut gates, ride round the edge of crops and stay off sidewalks/pavements, public footpaths and private land.

In England and Wales, public rights of way are paths on which the public have a legally protected right to pass and re-pass. Both walkers and cyclists, as well as horses, are allowed on bridleways, and riders can also use byways.

You can ride on tree lawns or road verges providing there are no signs prohibiting it. Keep an eye out for drainage ditches, rabbit holes, molehills, boggy ground and discarded bottles and other trash that might startle your horse or cause injury.

When riding through wooded areas, look out for low-hanging branches and hidden tree roots and allow your horse to pick his own way through water.

In the UK, if your local bridleway becomes dangerous or impassable – perhaps it is blocked by a tree, is water-logged, bordered by a bird scarer or impeded by electric or barbed wire fencing, inform your local authority's rights of way department.

Does your horse become over-excited on a ride? Exuberant horses often benefit from being turned out, schooled or longed/lunged before hacking out. If you school while out hacking, it will help to concentrate your horse's mind on work and not play. So your horse doesn't anticipate going faster, try to vary the spots where you canter, approach from another direction or go on an entirely different route altogether. Riding out with a bombproof horse may also have a comfort blanket effect!

Safe not sorry

For safety's sake when riding on UK roads, always familiarize yourself with the Highway Code and follow this advice:

1. When riding on a public highway, children under 14 must legally wear a helmet that complies with current safety standards and is securely fastened. But it goes without saying, anyone riding a horse should always wear a helmet conforming to the latest safety standards, whether it's hacking along a road or schooling in an enclosed area.

2. When leading a horse, keep him on your left.

3. Bear in mind that when riding on the roads, conditions and situations can change very quickly. Remember that plastic paint – used for white lines and zebra crossings – and worn, shiny patches on roads can be slippery, as are corners – so don't trot around them! Grit or dirt provides a safer footing.

QUICK T!P

THE END OF THE RIDE

On returning, don't just untack and leave your horse in his stable or chuck him in the field. Give him a rub down or hose him if he's hot and sweaty. Massage his back briskly to help restore circulation. And always ensure you offer him a drink of fresh water.

Show Time

> *If your horse says no, you either asked the wrong question or asked the question wrong.*

Pat Parelli

Chapter 5
Show Time

Showing can be great fun, providing you always put your horse's comfort first – if it's a hot day, stand him in the shade and ensure he has access to water at all times. Remember – it's the taking part, not the winning that counts – you will always come home with the best horse, even if you're rosette-less!

Boxing clever

Always have your showing 'box of tricks' fully stocked and to hand at a show. Re-pack and check the contents the night before – it'll save you time on show mornings:

- Braiding/plaiting gear – needle, thread and scissors or rubber bands

- Equine and human first aid kits

- Sweatpants/tracksuit bottoms/trackies and T-shirt or overalls to keep your show clothes clean

- Studs

- Spare hairnet

- Boot polish

- Cash for emergencies

- Bottle of water to keep you hydrated

- Your cell phone/mobile

"There is something about jumping a horse over a fence, something that makes you feel good. Perhaps it's the risk, the gamble. In any event it's a thing I need."

William Faulkner

Wash and go!

Bathing, grooming and braiding/plaiting are all necessary chores if you want your horse to look his best in the ring and impress the judges.

A few days before the show, bathe your horse with equine shampoo, not dishwashing/washing up liquid as it is too harsh, especially for grays and chestnuts who tend to have more sensitive skin. With a new shampoo, try it on a small patch on the neck and leave for 24 hours to ensure your horse isn't allergic to it. Remember to rinse shampoo out thoroughly as any residue can encourage dandruff and itching.

To remove the last residue of grease after bathing, put a double handful of washing soda/soda crystals in half a bucket of warm water, wring out an old dish towel/tea towel and rub it over your horse's body in sweeping circular strokes.

Bathing benefits

Bathing your horse can help to:

- Get rid of any loose hairs if he is changing his coat

- Eradicate any parasites or skin complaints with the aid of a medical or herbal shampoo

- Stimulate circulation and act as a form of massage

- Make your horse feel and look good

- Properly remove dulling grease and dust from the coat.

Choose a warm day to bathe your horse, and use an anti-sweat sheet (a horsey string vest!) or cooler blanket/rug made from material that wicks away moisture to help him dry off afterwards. But if you can at all avoid it, don't bathe your horse in winter as he'll need the natural oils in his coat for protection against the elements.

Braiding for beginners

Turnout for both horse and rider is very important, whatever the level of competition.

So when it comes to braiding/plaiting manes and tails, practice definitely makes perfect.

Don't wash the mane and tail immediately before a show as this makes the hair too slippery to braid/plait. A few days in advance, pull the mane so it's tidy and easier to braid/plait. Pull hairs from underneath, especially if the mane tends to lie on the wrong side of the neck or stick up, to a length of 10-13cm (4-5in). Pull the mane after exercise when your horse is still warm as the hairs will come out more easily while the pores are open.

Problems with a greasy mane and/or tail? Then dampen a clean cloth with rubbing alcohol/surgical spirit or Witch Hazel astringent (UK) and rub it over the hair.

Before braiding/plaiting, brush or comb the mane thoroughly then 'lay' it with a damp brush (using sugar and water mixed together is said to help lay the mane flat) to tame stray strands and hold the braids/plaits in place while the hair dries. If dandruff is a problem, make sure you wet the mane more, so you can flick out any dry, scaly bits.

Divide the mane into equal sections, using rubber bands, and dampen again if necessary. Clothes pegs or bulldog clips are useful if you prefer to keep the rest of the mane out of the way while you're braiding/plaiting. And remember to braid/plait on the off side (right) of your horse's neck – the side the judges will notice first!

Applying egg white, styling gel or setting lotion to the mane before braiding/plaiting is a cheap and easy way to stop split ends from sticking out and will bind broken hairs, plus it makes it easier for you to keep the braids/plaits tight.

Using a needle and cotton of a similar color to your horse's mane, rather than rubber bands, will give a more professional appearance. It's perhaps a good idea not to use a needle and thread in the stable due to the lack of natural light and the fact you may drop the needle – bringing a whole new, relevant meaning to finding a needle in a haystack!

Don't be tempted to cut off wispy bits of hair afterwards – hairspray, mousse or gel is a much better taming tactic!

Some dressage riders prefer to use white tape around the braids/plaits because they think it helps highlight the horse's top line and makes the neck stand out, especially if it's well-muscled.

Braiding by numbers

The round 'button' braids/plaits are most commonly seen in both American and British show rings. Always aim for an odd number of braids/plaits, excluding the forelock – seven for a pony; nine, 11 or 13 for a horse. If your horse has a short neck, you may find using 13 small braids/plaits will give him a more swan-like appearance. Using fewer, larger braids/plaits on a long-necked horse creates the opposite effect. Remember, though, that too many tiny braids/plaits can look fussy while too few thick braids/plaits may resemble a row of golf balls!

Another popular braiding/plaiting trick is to give a thin-necked horse a deeper, more muscled appearance by placing the braids/plaits on the crest of the neck, rather than to the side. Thick necks benefit from the opposite treatment. For a tidier forelock, try putting it into a French (or Andalusian) braid/plait instead of an ordinary one.

Style 'n set

Even if it means an early start, always try to braid/plait on the morning of the show. Although you may think you're saving time the night before, you risk the braids/plaits looking messy the following day and having to be re-done anyway. Also, leaving the braids/plaits in overnight can pull the hair out and make the neck sore – not ideal if you want your horse to work loosely and comfortably in the ring. Leave his forelock to the last minute so he is less likely to rub it.

Keep an old pantyhose/pair of tights handy to protect braids/plaits from hay and dust – secure them over each one with an elastic band.

If your horse has rubbed his braids/plaits and split the hairs just before you go into the ring, undo the braid/plait and apply a strong hair gel before re-braiding/plaiting.

Baby oil applied just before you go into the ring will make the braids/plaits glisten.

To remove braids/plaits afterwards, use a dressmaker's stitch unpicker as scissors can damage the hair.

Braid-me-beautiful

For breeds with long, flowing manes like Arabs and Andalusians or for horses with very thick manes, a decorative Spanish or running braid/plait can help keep the mane both neat and attractive-looking.

For a Spanish braid/plait, part the mane down the center so that an equal amount of hair falls down each side of the neck, and braid/plait each side along the crest.

A running braid/plait uses a similar method but it curves down and round instead.

A likely tail

As with the mane, your horse's tail should be pulled and washed a few days before braiding/plaiting – and the end trimmed too.

Before pulling the tail, ask someone to hold the horse's head and back him up to a closed stable door. Then you can stand on the other side without fear of getting kicked.

Wearing surgical gloves or a pair of lightweight rubber gloves when pulling your horse's tail will guard against blisters and will give you a better grip on the hair.

Pull your horse's tail from underneath at the top, working mainly to the sides, keeping both sides even.

Trim the tail so it hangs down to the point of the hock or slightly below when the horse is carrying it (10cm/4in below the hock at rest). If your horse has straight hocks, a long tail can emphasize this weakness. Try shortening the tail to just below the hock's chestnut, in order to draw the judge's attention upwards to the point of his hock. For horses with poor hocks, allow a little more length for extra coverage.

Using clippers – instead of scissors – can give a cleaner line and smarter finish to the end of a tail.

Apply a tail bandage for short periods each day until the show to help flatten the hair and train the shape of the tail.

When braiding/plaiting, only take a few hairs from the side each time as too many will make your center braid/plait look bulky.

Make a thin tail look wavy and full by braiding/plaiting it when it is still wet after washing. Unbraid/plait when it's dry, and comb through with your fingers, not a brush as this will break the hairs.

An all-round trim

Trimming your horse's legs and under his jaw with clippers helps give a neat outline – but if he is slightly light of bone, don't trim down the back of his legs as you'll accentuate this defect.

When trimming fetlocks and the hair around the coronet band, use scissors with rounded ends for a more professional – and safe – finish. Trimming combs with a replaceable razor blade screwed in over the teeth (used by dog groomers) can be quite handy for this job as well.

Tidy traveler

If your horse is an inexperienced traveler, practice loading and unloading in the weeks and days leading up to the show. Drive round the block, slowly increasing the time he is on board.

For horses who tend to sweat up while traveling, use a cooler blanket/rug rather than a string-type anti-sweat sheet as the latter will leave his coat imprinted with its pattern.

An old pantyhose/pair of tights will come in handy to use over a braided/plaited tail, under a bandage, to protect your handiwork and keep it clean while en route. When taking the bandage off, remember to unwind rather than pull from the top!

Safe landing!

On arriving at the show, park in a shady area on level ground – take a block of wood in case you need to level up the ramp.

Having unloaded your horse, wipe denatured alcohol (methylated spirits) over his body with a cloth to get rid of the dust from the journey and to give his coat a professional shine.

If your horse is fussy and won't drink water away from home, either take supplies from the barn/yard or try adding a little peppermint cordial to the water.

First show? The traditional way of warning fellow competitors that your horse is a novice is by tying a green ribbon round his tail. Similarly, a red ribbon signifies that your horse is known to kick.

Tack tips

Consider how your tack will suit your horse at a show: a fine head tends to look its best in a thin, lightweight bridle while more workmanlike gear with a wider noseband would look better on a cob.

A straight-cut saddle will show off your horse's shoulder more – but make sure the seat is comfortable for both you and the judge! Remember that a high pommel, for instance, will not go down so well with a male judge, while a larger framed judge may not appreciate a tiny seat! If you're small-framed it might be worth using a saddle that's slightly too big for you (but still fits your horse well) so it's more likely to be comfortable for the judge – use bigger stirrup irons and longer leathers, too.

Avoid oversized or badly fitting saddle pads/numnahs as they can spoil the overall effect of your turnout. The professionals use pure sheepskin saddle pads/numnahs that fit the saddle exactly and do not move or slip.

Always introduce new pieces of tack – particularly bits – at home first.

If performing a dressage test in the UK, a hunting breastplate can give the impression that your horse has a rounder neck and can help break up big shoulders for horses who tend to go on to the forehand.

When using a double or full bridle (consisting of a curb – or Weymouth bit and a snaffle – bridoon/bradoon), which is compulsory at advanced level dressage, ensure you twist the curb chain clockwise so that all the links are lying flat, before fastening it. Then thread the thin leather lip strap, which is designed to keep the curb chain still, through a separate link in the middle and buckle on the near side of the bit, in the metal loop above the bottom ring of the curb.

Tricks of the trade

Keep spent matchsticks handy for getting saddle soap out of the holes in stirrup leathers and other hard-to-reach places.

If you're using studs for extra grip in a competition, clean out the holes in your horse's shoes with a horseshoe nail the night before and pack them with cotton wool dipped in oil or petroleum jelly. This helps the cotton wool stay in place and keeps the holes rust-free. A pair of point-nosed tweezers will come in handy for pulling the cotton wool out. Not only will this routine save you time on the day – no scraping out dirt when you're in a hurry to load up – but it will make fitting the studs easier.

QUICK T!P
BLEMISH BUSTERS!
Boot polish is the tried and tested old-fashioned way to hide blemishes (scars or white hairs) on a dark horse's coat; chalk or talcum powder for marks on a gray and shoe whitener to brighten up socks. Plus there is now a bewildering choice of horsey makeup on the market for this specific purpose.

Dress to impress

Don't forget that the smallest detail can count and make all the difference.

Buying the best jacket you can afford will enhance your appearance no end. Try and match the colors of your show shirt and tie with your horse's browband.

Store your helmet away from direct sunlight to prevent it fading – ideally use a purpose-made hat bag, and just before a show, hold a velvet-covered helmet over the steam from a boiling kettle to raise the nap of the material and make it look like new. A suede shoe spray of the appropriate color can help lift tired or worn velvet helmets.

With rubber riding boots, use a little furniture polish from an aerosol for a dazzling shine.

For extra neatness, trim off the corners of your number. Rounded edges are also less likely to curl up.

Pop the flower for your button hole in some damp paper towel/kitchen roll, wrapped with foil, in the fridge overnight to keep it fresh and prevent it from opening further.

Girls! Don't wear too much make-up for a showing class – less is more!

And never under-estimate the power of wearing a smile – whatever discipline you are doing – at least the judge will think you are enjoying yourself, which is after all, what it's all about!

Finishing touches

Disposable razors are handy for removing the whiskers around your horse's muzzle – although some owners don't like doing this because horses use their whiskers to gauge distances. However, particularly for horses that lack breeding, removing the whiskers and adding a dash of baby oil to the muzzle, eye area, chestnuts and under the tail, can inject a touch of class.

If applying coat gloss to give your horse that final overall shine, remember not to use it on the saddle area as it could cause the saddle to slip. Be warned that coat conditioner can make your reins slippery too!

Keep some adhesive tape handy for removing hairs from your clothes and your horse's saddle pad/numnah.

Just before you jump on board, apply hoof oil so it looks fresh and you're less likely to mess up your clean show clothes. Even ensure the soles of your boots are clean!

In fact, it makes sense to wear an old pair of sweatpants/trackies and T-shirt or overalls over your show clothes, which can be stripped off just before you climb on board and ride into the ring – thereby keeping any smears or stains to a minimum. That's unless you are lucky enough to have a groom or helper on hand to do all your dirty work for you, of course!

If you have a young horse who is bothered by the noise at competitions, cut down some sponges and insert the pieces in his ears.

Be nice

Always be courteous to your fellow competitors and consider their needs as well as your own – don't hog the practice fence for longer than necessary and don't get too close to other riders' horses.

When parking your trailer or lorry, leave ample space between yours and the next vehicle to allow for horses to be tied up and ramps lowered.

Why not offer to help higher or lower practice poles for your fellow competitors once you've finished in the ring? You never know when you might need their help in the future!

Keep your cool

So you've got to the show and both you and your horse are looking your best. Now all you have to do is compete!

Sounds easy – unless you feel like you're having a panic attack! Nerves affect us all – even the top riders have butterflies and some adrenaline is a good thing. Breathing slowly and deeply can help slow your heart rate. Take a quiet moment to close your eyes and picture yourself performing a perfect dressage test or jumping a clear round – always expect the best, not fear the worst.

QUICK T!P
STAY CALM!
Does your horse fidget and refuse to stand quietly in line while the judges make their decision? Then distract him by scratching very hard just below his withers, or by pinching a fold of his skin.

In the clear

If you've entered a showjumping class, here are a few tips to help you remember the course and to boost your confidence…

1. Arrive early so you are not flustered from the start. Find a plan of the course and concentrate on walking the exact route you plan to take. Walk through the start – many riders don't do this – and look for your approach into the first fence, then the second, as you will need to be thinking about this as you land. After every three or four fences, stop and retrace your steps so they become entrenched in your mind.

2. Walk the course at least twice, and ideally, have a more experienced rider with you. Don't be afraid to ask a professional if you can walk round with them – most are happy to share their expertise.

3. With any tricky doubles, combinations or related distances, stride them out and remember to walk through the finish.

4. Talking yourself round the course – "one is the upright; two the parallel; three the rustic" etc. – may also help you remember the route.

5. If you have the luxury of being placed down the order, it will help you to watch the first few riders' rounds to remind you of the route and to see if there are any particular fences that cause problems.

6. Don't forget, if the show operates a flag system, red is on your right (remember 'RR'!) and white is on your left.

7. Make a mental note of any changes to the going – areas where the ground may be wet, muddy or rough – so you can plan how to ride or avoid them.

Ways to warm up well

Start warming up your horse about 40 minutes – even longer if he's young – before it's your turn in the ring. To begin with, walk your horse quietly to settle him, get him used to the surroundings and to loosen his muscles.

Introduce trot and canter and do some suppling exercises such as leg yield and shoulder-in plus plenty of transitions. When your horse is ready, trot him over his first practice fence – a crosspole will encourage him to jump in the middle – two or three times before tackling a small upright in canter.

Start small and ask a helper to raise the fence gradually to build and keep both your own and your horse's confidence up.

When you are happy with the way your horse is going, progress to jumping first an ascending spread, increasing the height and width each time, then a parallel. If things go wrong, simply put the poles down a couple of notches and start again. If all is going well, you probably won't need to jump your horse more than eight times before going into the ring.

It's best to have made a good job of your last practice jump. Always remember to ride away from the fence – as if you were approaching the next one – so your horse doesn't get into the habit of switching off every time he lands.

And the best tip? Think positively! Always tell yourself you're going to do well before entering the ring. If you think you'll have a fence down, you probably will.

> **" When I'm approaching a water jump, with dozens of photographers waiting for me to fall in, and hundreds of spectators wondering what's going to happen next, the horse is just about the only one who doesn't know I am Royal! "**

The Princess Royal

Cross-country hang ups

Does your horse waver from water, dump you in ditches, baulk at banks or hurl you at hedges? Then only by practicing spooky fences at home will you overcome this particular hurdle – literally!

If your horse has a problem with water and your budget won't stretch to buying a water tray, improvise with blue plastic sheets laid on the ground. Concentrate on schooling your horse over a variety of home-made water-type obstacles in a balanced and forward canter. If necessary, follow an older, more experienced horse that's not likely to spook.

Is there a ford, stream or shallow, slow moving river with a firm bottom within hacking distance? Then walk your horse quietly into it, ideally following a reliable schoolmaster. Once the horse becomes more confident, progress to trot.

With ditches, approach in walk and give your horse time to look – rather like jockeys do with the first fence in a steeplechase. Use inviting 'tools' such as wings or a single rail to help guide the horse over the obstacle. Alternatively, find a shallow depression in the ground or a drainage ditch and walk your horse over it. If this causes a problem, lead him over first then ask a helper to lead him over with you on board.

Go cross-country schooling or book yourself onto a cross-country training clinic to introduce your horse to as wide a variety of fences as possible. Always aim to end the session on a good note.

And although it may be difficult at first, teach yourself not to concentrate on the problem fence – look over and away from it and think about the next obstacle.

Go West!

> *" The best horses are the best because they try harder. "*

Robert Smith

Chapter 6
Go West!

Western riding can trace its roots back to the Spanish conquistadors, who landed in the Americas in the early 1500s.

Their approach to riding, warfare and cattle-working was refined in the 1800s by cowboys on ranches throughout the 'wild west' of America. They needed horses, equipment and a way of riding that would enable them to spend long hours in the saddle, cope with rough terrain and rope, steer, brand and doctor cattle with efficiency, speed and skill.

This resulted in the development of neck reining (using one hand to control the horse with precision while the other lassoed a cow), functional and comfortable tack that minimized the risk of falling and injury and the fast and agile Quarter Horse, which can not only turn on a sixpence but is the quickest breed in the world over a quarter of a mile.

The great thing about Western riding is that it combines a laid-back approach with sophisticated, precise training and encompasses casual pleasure riding, functional farm or ranch work and highly competitive events or activities.

A growing number of enthusiasts all over the world enjoy competing in trail riding, showing, rodeo and pleasure riding while the sport of reining, which is very easy to learn but requires a high level of skill and dedication to master, has been approved by the international equestrian federation, the FEI.

Whatever your chosen Western riding discipline or activity, you don't have to be a professional cowboy or cowgirl to learn and enjoy it!

Tack tips

Check the quality of Western tack by ensuring that the stitching is straight and even, all seams and parts fit well and the edges are finished properly.

Bridles explained

Western bridles have a lot less leather 'furniture' than their English counterparts and often don't include a noseband unless they're a hackamore (bitless bridle), which is also known as a 'Jaquima'. Recognize a one-ear headstall, which complements a fine, pretty head, by its crownpiece, ear loop and sidepieces. A more secure browband headstall comprises sidepieces, a crownpiece, browband and throatlatch, and is suitable for any bit.

Bits range from a mild snaffle, which doesn't apply any leverage, to a more severe curb, which applies pressure to the horse's mouth, poll and chin groove via its shanks. Straight shanks can exert more leverage than a backward-curved shank.

Remember, if competing in a show event, a mechanical hackamore (which consists of a noseband with long metal shanks and a curb chain) is usually not permitted. However, these bridles are allowed in speed events and trail riding classes.

If you are using split reins, you can make adjustments with just your index finger placed between the reins. You don't need to have a finger between 'romal' reins (these are joined together at the end by a type of long quirt), which should have at least 16ins of slack between them.

Safe as saddles...

For the cowboy to do his job efficiently, safely and comfortably, it was important that the Western saddle had a high cantle (rear), deep seat, a substantial tree to provide support while roping and a prominent pommel or horn for the lasso. As the English style saddle has adapted to suit different sports and disciplines – general purpose, dressage, show, event and jumping saddles – so has the Western saddle. Decide which type is best for you, your horse and the choice of event:

- Barrel racing saddle – has a short, deep seat

- Cutting saddle – with a long, flat seat

- Pleasure saddle – complete with a decorative, comfortable seat

- Reiner saddle – has a higher cantle than the cutting saddle

- Roping/ranch saddle – lowest cantle of all the saddles

Western saddles are secured with two girths – a front cinch (cincha) and rear cinch. Choose a straight cinch for pleasure classes and a wider-coverage cinch for roping events.

Complementary extras

Protect your horse's back with a woven wool saddle blanket under the saddle. Double weave blankets are looser, softer and thicker than a single weave but are expensive and difficult to clean and dry. Therefore, it's a good idea to use a thin underpad – made from wool felt, foam, rubber or gel with a canvas or wool cover – under the blanket to keep it clean.

There is a wide range of stirrups designed to accompany particular styles of Western saddle. Choose from:

- A leather 'Visalia' style stirrup with silver trim for a pleasure saddle

- A varnished oak 'Visalia' style reining stirrup for a reiner saddle

- A heavy roping stirrup for a roping/ranch saddle, which allows the rider to get out of the saddle quickly

- A thin steel oxbow stirrup covered in rawhide, leather or silver with a rounded bottom, for a cutting saddle.

Web halters – similar to those in the UK – are usually made of nylon webbing with heavy brass or chrome-plated buckles, and are used for everyday activities like leading, tying up and grooming. A knotted rope halter has no metal buckles and can act as a training aid, while a Western show halter is made of leather with silver trim and buckles. Reserved purely for the show ring, it's used with a chain shank threaded under the horse's jaw.

A tiedown is a more severe variation of the standing martingale, and is sometimes seen in Western riding disciplines. It is adjusted much shorter than a standing martingale and aims to prevent the horse from flipping his head up when asked to stop abruptly or to turn at speed. One end of this adjustable strap attaches to the horse's breastplate and the other to a rope or leather noseband. When the horse raises his head above the desired point, the slack is taken out of the strap and pressure is placed on his nose.

Boots are very important for protecting a horse's legs against bangs and knocks, especially in speed competitions. Splint boots, which include a hard strike plate, guard the inside of the front cannon bones against injuries caused by the opposite leg. Stretchy neoprene support or sport boots provide elastic support to the flexor tendons, although these boots aren't permitted in all classes. Bell boots – similar to overreach boots in the UK – are sometimes worn on either the front feet or all four feet to protect the pastern, coronary band and bulbs of the heel from being caught by other hooves. They are not permitted in most show ring classes but are popular in barrel racing, timed events and reining. Skid or run-down boots fasten over the rear fetlocks to prevent friction burns during high-speed events such as reining, cutting or roping, when the horse has to stop deep and hard.

Dressed for success

Appearance is very important in Western riding events. If competing in rodeo, cutting or reining, then practical Western work attire should be worn. This typically consists of a long-sleeved shirt, felt or straw wide-brimmed cowboy hat, jeans and cowboy boots, often complemented by chaps, a neckerchief, spurs, decorative belt and gloves. Show attire is reserved for some competitive show events and is a lot flashier.

Natural or pulled?

When considering whether to leave your horse's mane and/or tail long or to pull/trim the hair, it depends what discipline or classes you plan to take part in. For horsemanship and pleasure classes, any style of mane is permitted while the tail should be left full. To increase the fullness or length of your horse's tail, use horse-hair hanks as tail extensions.

For reining and cutting competitions, keep the mane long with the tail ending half way down the cannon bones, so it doesn't get trodden on when the horse performs a rein-back.

Meanwhile, in roping and timed events, a short mane and tapered tail will guard against the hair getting tangled up in tack or other equipment.

Sitting pretty

In Western riding, the five aids are the mind, upper body, base (seat, back, thighs and weight), lower legs and hands.

When aboard, remember to relax. Your position should be natural, consistent and secure with a flat and supple back while your seat and inner thighs should be in close contact with the saddle. Keep your shoulders level and square and your heels down with a slight bend at the knees – the stirrup length is even longer than that for dressage. The arm holding the reins should be bent at the elbow with the hand above or slightly in front of the saddle horn. Keep your free hand either straight or bent at the elbow so it doesn't touch either the horse or equipment.

Common Western riding faults include slouching instead of sitting upright, hands that are either too high or too low, feet stuck too far forward so it looks like the rider is sitting on a chair rather than standing up, and toes pointing downwards or too far outwards.

Starting off

To ask the horse to move forwards, simply squeeze with both legs at the cinch and keep a light contact on both reins.

When neck reining, your reining hand mustn't cross more than a few inches over the horse's withers. To turn right, move your reining hand slightly to the right so that the left rein touches the horse's neck and he moves away from this slight pressure – vice versa to move left.

Your inside leg helps create and maintain the bend while the outside leg controls the horse's hindquarters when turning or on a circle.

In English riding, the gaits are walk, trot, canter and gallop but in Western, the gaits are walk (a natural four-footed four-beat gait), jog (a smooth, even and rhythmical two-beat diagonal gait, which the rider sits to), lope (an easy three-beat gait), extended jog (when the horse takes a longer – not quicker – stride) and gallop or run (a four-beat accelerated lope with increased impulsion and length of stride).

During training sessions, perform simple exercises well, smoothly and off both the left and right rein first before moving on to more complicated movements or introducing speed – aim to work the horse off his hindquarters and keep an even rhythm. Think relaxed yet energized.

If working in an enclosed arena, ride on the inside track so that the horse responds to your aids, not the rails or fence.

Practice lots of straight lines (ensuring that your horse's body isn't at an angle and that his hind feet follow the tracks of his front feet), circles (use a cone to help you ride evenly) for improving straightness, lateral work and collection, and spirals to help gather the horse and shift his weight onto his quarters. A good exercise is a figure-8, when instead of crossing diagonally in an X shape, you ride straight across the center line.

Maneuvers include leg yielding (moving forward on a straight line while stepping sideways with the hind legs), turn on the forehand (when the quarters rotate around the forehand), sidepass (stepping sideways while keeping the body straight), rein back (a two-beat diagonal gait in reverse), turn on the hindquarters (when the forehand moves around the hind end), pivot (a 90° or 180° turn on the hindquarters from a standstill) and collection (asking the horse to work with his quarters under him, such as jog-walk-stop-back-jog transitions to help improve balance).

Ringing the changes

There is a wide range of competitions for the Western rider to choose from. Here's a quick round-up…

- Western pleasure – showing the horse with others at walk, jog and canter. The judge will look for balanced, smooth and correct gaits, good control on a loose rein with a low head carriage and almost invisible aids and minimal interference from the rider.

- Trail class – this tests a horse's reaction and coordination to obstacles that would be encountered on a ranch or trail, such as bridges, gates, log jams and flapping objects. The judge pays close attention to the horse's performance, manners, response to the rider, quality of movement and ability to perform intricate maneuvers in tight spaces – although speed isn't judged, partnerships have a time limit for completing each obstacle.

- Reining – viewed as the 'dressage' of Western riding, this discipline requires a horse and rider to perform a precise pattern that consists of circles at lope and gallop with flying changes of lead, rapid spins (a turn in one spot on the haunches), rollbacks (a rapid turn immediately followed by a gallop in the opposite direction) and sliding stops (stopping from a full gallop) with balance and fluidity.

- Cutting – this cattle event requires the horse and rider to select and separate a cow from the herd. Then the rider relaxes the reins and trusts the horse to use his 'cow sense' to prevent the animal from returning to the others. Depending on the level of competition, between one and three judges award marks.

- Working cow horse or reined cow horse – rather like a cross between cutting and reining, this competition involves the horse and rider working a single cow in a directed way through several maneuvers.

- Ranch horse – an event that tests multiple categories used by working ranch horses, such as ranch riding (similar to Western pleasure), ranch trail (a range of testing tasks, often judged on natural terrain rather than in an arena), ranch cutting (judged in the same way as a cutting event), working ranch horse (reining, roping and working cow horse) and ranch conformation (judged in the same way as a halter class).

- Western riding – a pattern class that combines elements of Western pleasure, reining and trail. The horse has to negotiate a gate, jog over a pole and lope through cones while demonstrating eight flying lead changes, a sliding stop and a rein back. The judges look for smooth gaits, responsiveness, manners and disposition.

- Team penning – a timed event in which a team of three riders must select between three and five marked cows from a herd and drive them into a small pen, shutting the gate once they have corralled all the designated cattle. The fastest team wins and those who exceed the time limit are disqualified. A similar event to this is ranch sorting.

- Halter, conformation or breeding classes – the horse's conformation and movement are judged in these in-hand classes.

- Halter showmanship, showmanship at halter, youth showmanship, showmanship in-hand or fitting and showmanship – in these classes, it is the handler's performance that is assessed, along with the

cleanliness of the horse and equipment, the handler's attire and the horse's behavior. The competitor is judged on their ability to fit and present the halter horse at his best as well as taking the horse through a short pattern at walk and jog with turns, while pivoting and backing up in more advanced classes.

- Western equitation, Western horsemanship, stock seat equitation or reining seat equitation – this tests the rider's ability to ride with precision, smoothness and balance. Competitors must perform a pattern or test in walk, jog and lope off both reins at the judge's discretion. Their position, control of the horse and accuracy and smoothness of movements are judged – not the horse's conformation or training. Remember, you must hold the reins with one hand if using a curb bit but two hands are allowed with a snaffle bit or hackamore (the latter is only permitted for use on young or 'junior' horses). Both split and romal reins are allowed but horses can't wear a noseband or cavesson or any type of protective boot or bandage unless performing a reining pattern.

- Rodeo – this hugely entertaining and crowd-pleasing sporting contest tests the skill and speed of the cowboy in events like tie-down or calf roping, team roping, steer wrestling, saddle bronc riding, bareback bronc riding, bull riding, barrel racing and pole bending. Rodeo is the official state sport of Wyoming, South Dakota and Texas but is banned in the UK and Holland.

Tail End

" If your horse doesn't care, you shouldn't either. "

Linsay Lee

Chapter 7
Tail End

Getting hitched

Towing a trailer or driving a truck/lorry requires skill, awareness and confidence even without a horse being on board. If you're a trailer towing virgin, why not book yourself onto a specialist course? In the UK, various companies organize these – visit www.learners.co.uk/towing for more information.

For British drivers who passed their car driving test on or after January 1 1997, they may need to pass a separate towing test to tow a travel trailer/caravan weighing more than 750kg MAM (Maximum Authorised Mass). To drive a vehicle over 3500kg (3.5 tonnes), it's necessary to pass a test for medium-sized goods vehicles.

If you passed your test before January 1997, you can drive a vehicle up to 7,500kg (7.5 tonnes).

Speed control

When towing on single carriageway de-restricted roads in the UK, remember the maximum speed limit is 50mph, while on dual carriageways and highways/motorways, the maximum limit is 60mph.

Courtesy cars!

The longer the distance you need to travel, the more chance a queue of slow moving traffic will build up behind you, especially if much of your route involves narrow roads or country lanes. Be considerate – pull over into a turnout, passing place or lay-by when it's safe to do so, to let cars pass you.

Get into gear

Before towing your horse in the UK, especially in winter, you'll need to plan well ahead. Don't forget:

- To fill up with gas/fuel, and check the oil, battery and water levels, as well as tire tread, pressure and brakes. Also top up your vehicle's windscreen washer and cooling system with antifreeze, to avoid burst radiators, split hoses and cracked engine blocks.

- To check your load distribution (aim for 50-75kg on the drawbar) and coupling height.

- To make sure lights, electrics and indicators are working; the trailer's jockey wheel or prop stand is fully wound up and secure; the correct license plate is fitted to the rear; the breakaway cable is connected and the trailer is safely coupled with everything inside properly secured.

- To ensure that the flooring is safe – look out for any signs of rotting or dampness underneath rubber mats.

- A flashlight/torch with batteries that work, plus some spares.

- A charged cell phone/mobile containing the numbers of your vet and barn/yard.

- Extra food and water for both you and your horse, in case you get held up.

- A section of old carpet, stored in the trunk/boot of your car, to use under your vehicle's wheels should you get stuck in mud or snow.

- A warning triangle, in case you break down.

- Human and equine first aid kits.

- Blankets/rugs for your horse.

- All the necessary documents, such as breakdown cover, contact number, and your horse's passport.

- Sunglasses – in case a rare ray of sun threatens to dazzle you!

- De-icer and windscreen scraper.

- A map and detailed directions or GNSS/satnav so you're not so reliant on reading road signs in bad weather.

- A small fire extinguisher, kept in your car.

Going backwards

Learning to reverse a trailer is one of the trickiest aspects of towing, but with lots of practice in a flat empty field or parking lot, you'll soon master it. Start off slowly and steadily by reversing in a straight line before progressing to backing round a corner. You'll need to steer your vehicle in the opposite direction to normal.

Place your hand/hands at the bottom of the steering wheel, keep them there and do not move them at any cost. Looking behind you, move your hand/s in the same direction you want the back corner of the trailer to turn. Start off slowly until you get the hang of it.

Putting out markers in a paddock, or even better, a disused airfield or parking lot, to replicate gateways and narrow roads/lanes will be less stressful and safer than practicing on busy streets or roads.

On the road

If you are traveling with a single horse in a trailer, he should always stand on the driver's side (off side in the UK and near side in the US) to counteract the camber of the road and for a smoother ride.

When towing, never descend a hill with the gearbox in neutral, as the vehicle will run away quickly, greatly increasing the risk of you losing control.

After traveling a few miles, stop somewhere safe, such as a rest area. Walk round the trailer to see that everything is still OK – check the tire pressure, ensure the coupling and safety chains are still fastened, that the lights are working and that everything remains properly secured. If you're traveling a long distance, have a rest break every two to three hours to run through these points, check your horse over and offer him some water.

If traveling with one horse alone in a truck or lorry, it's best if he stands as far forward as possible.

Always make a note of the height and weight of your truck/lorry in case you encounter low bridges or ones with weight restrictions.

A head start

Before traveling with your horse, he'll need to be kitted out in certain gear to help guard against bumps and knocks while he's in transit. One such item is a poll guard, to ensure the sensitive area between his ears is protected. Threading the headpiece of his halter/headcollar through an old sponge will do this job just as effectively.

Going round in circles

Need to exercise your horse but don't have the time? Then longeing/lungeing – using a long rein from the ground – is ideal for helping maintain your horse's fitness, as well as benefiting balance and rhythm, correcting bad habits, increasing suppleness, settling an over-fresh horse before he's ridden and varying routine.

You can longe/lunge in a bridle or halter/headcollar but a longe/lunge cavesson is best. Start with five minutes on each rein and build up to 20-30 minutes in total. This is the equivalent of schooling your horse for an hour.

Work your horse for a few minutes on each rein before adding side reins, attached to the saddle or a roller, to give him the chance to stretch and relax.

QUICK T!P
SPACE PLATFORM
If you don't have access to an arena, longe/lunge your horse using a flat corner of an empty field (at least 20m × 20m), which is neither slippery nor hard and has good going. Enclose the open sides with poles, barrels or straw bales so that your horse is less likely to be distracted.

Troubleshooting

Does your horse tend to turn in on the circle and face you? Then pointing the longe/lunge whip at his shoulder and showing positive body language should help discourage him from doing this.

If your horse won't slow down when you ask, try altering your body language. Simply turning your body slightly away from the horse and dropping your eyes can have the desired effect.

Banishing boredom

So that your horse doesn't become bored on the longe/lunge and to improve his balance, try introducing transitions, ever decreasing circles and extension and collection.

Vary the exercise further by adding poles – in a fan shape if you want him to tackle them on the circle or run alongside him in a straight line – to help boost his athleticism.

Pole position

When longeing/lungeing over poles, gauge your horse's stride and check distances by ensuring that his hind foot lands exactly half way between the poles. For a 12.2hh pony, the distance between each pole should be no less than 1m 15cm (3ft 9in); 1m 20cm (4ft) for a 14.2hh; 1m 36cm (4ft 6in) for a 15.2hh and 1m 52cm (5ft) for a 16hh-plus.

QUICK T!P

OTHER EXERCISE ALTERNATIVES…

Groundwork training such as leading your horse through a home-made obstacle course or long reining can also be useful ways of exercising your horse, especially in winter.

Crossing boundaries

Ladder reins are a really good teaching aid for both beginners and disabled riders, as the leather 'steps' demonstrate how and where riders should hold the reins.

Rubber reins with colored sections are not only good for teaching disabled riders and beginners where to hold the reins, but help those of us who confuse left with right! Different colored gloves are also good for this.

Dressage

Not for nothing is the graceful and elegant art of dressage known as 'ballet on horseback'. Whether you are riding at preliminary or Grand Prix level, always aim to achieve the following six goals in your training: Suppleness, rhythm, contact, straightness, impulsion and collection.

Wear dark rather than light-colored gloves to deflect the judge's attention away from your hands.

Side-saddle

For hundreds of years, riding side-saddle was considered the only way for ladies to travel on horseback. Its popularity in Europe declined following the Second World War but has since been revived.

If you and your horse have reached a certain level in one discipline and are unlikely to progress further – or are just plain bored with riding astride – give the sport a go!

Because both of your legs are on the near (left) side of the horse, avoid bad habits like allowing your left heel to creep up. Sit still, straight and square, with your shoulders level and your right toe and left heel down.

Another tip is to try and keep your right thigh in contact with the saddle, thereby transferring your weight further forward – rising trot is a good exercise for this.

And if you feel brave enough to try jumping side-saddle, fold your body forward – rather than out of the saddle – as you go over the fence, moving towards your horse's right ear as this will counteract a natural tendency for you to be thrown to the left.

Driving

For those who prefer to follow a horse rather than be on one, driving is the ideal solution! However, a horse must always wear blinkers when he's being driven so he can't see the carriage 'following' him and be distracted or spooked.

For safety's sake, always have someone holding the horse's head when you get in or out of the carriage, and never take a bridle off while the horse is still attached to the carriage.

Endurance

The equine equivalent of running a marathon, endurance or trail riding is reserved for those of us with stamina and resilient rear ends who love spending hours (and hours and hours…!) in the saddle.

If you want to have a go at a novice endurance event, first ensure both you and your horse are fit enough to take part. As a rough guide, you need to build up to one hour's riding every day for five or six days a week over several weeks, to be able to cope with a 30-50km (20-30 mile) ride. Remember to increase the time gradually and make good use of any hills nearby to boost fitness levels.

Showjumping

Once mastered, showjumping is one of the most rewarding and satisfying equestrian sports: there are always bigger and more tricky fences and combinations to tackle – in a time faster than anyone else. The bar is always being raised – literally!

If you're not used to riding with shorter stirrups, practice by leaning against a wall with your legs at right angles. It hurts, but it helps build up your leg muscles and strengthen them for the jumping position.

When learning to jump, your instructor will probably tell you to practice the jumping position – folding forwards from the hips with your buttocks out of the saddle and the weight in your heels – in walk, trot and canter first, before progressing to tackling trotting poles and finally, a small crosspole. It takes budding showjumpers a while to learn how to spot a stride, but it comes with practice.

Eventing

Probably the most adrenaline-fueled of all equestrian sports, riding cross-country requires high levels of skill, accuracy and bravery.

When tackling any level of event, remember that changing light conditions can cause even straightforward obstacles to appear spooky to your horse, particularly when riding from light into shade. Sit up, encourage your horse onto as straight a line as possible and ride forward with plenty of impulsion – not speed as this will give your horse's eyes even less time to adjust.

Eventing tack tips

To prevent the saddle from slipping across country, sew a chamois leather cloth (or 'shammy') to the saddle pad/numnah. And don't forget a breastplate!

Tie the crownpiece/headstall (US) or headpiece (UK) of the bridle to the first braid/plait, so if you fall off you won't take the bridle with you!

Exercising eventing caution

With a young horse, it might be better to trot, rather than canter, the last few strides into a water obstacle. Launching into it might frighten your horse and cause him to refuse next time.

Avoid picking up a tendon injury at the end of your round by not stopping suddenly at the finish. Either slow down gradually or ride a few circles to keep the momentum going.

Good breeding

The decision to breed from your horse must never be taken lightly as it requires a great deal of knowledge and experience. There is simply no point breeding from a horse with a poor temperament and/or conformation.

When looking for a stallion to cover your mare, avoid butch, oversized individuals to limit the risk of a coarse foal with a lack of agility. Look for an athletic, balanced stallion who moves well, has good carriage and a kind eye. His conformation should include short cannon bones and flat bones, well-formed feet, a good neck and head set on a fine throat and good length in the hindquarters.

Foal's gold

So your mare has finally given birth and you're the proud owner of a bouncing filly or colt? The first few hours of a foal's life are critical. Check

his navel often – it should be clean and healthy, while the cord should dry up and eventually drop off.

Colostrum, the first milk from the mare, is vital for the foal because the antibodies it contains kick-start his immune system. If he doesn't receive colostrum within the first 12-36 hours of life, he'll become weak and sickly and perhaps die. Keep a close eye on him during this time.

Mare and foal may look the picture of health and happiness now, but when should you start to think about weaning?

Start reducing the mare's grain/concentrates when the foal is aged three months and is grazing well, to help her milk dry up and encourage the foal to eat alternative feed more readily. Ensure you step up the foal's grain/concentrates at the same time.

Wean the foal when he's at least six months old and is eating grass, hay and weaning nuts – his large intestine must be able to cope with fully digestible fibrous feed.

Five days before and after weaning, introduce probiotics to the foal's diet to minimize stress and prevent scouring.

You can either wean slowly – taking the foal away from the mare for an increasing amount of time each day – or separate them and keep them apart so they can't see or hear each other.

It will help if the foal has some company – ideally another foal, but otherwise any animal will do.

Give seaweed to both mare and foal as this is an excellent source of organic calcium.

Against
the Clock

" There's something about the outside of a horse that's good for the inside of a man. "

Sir Winston Churchill

Chapter 8
Against the Clock

There's always so much to do and so little time when it comes to horses. Here are some time-saving tips to give you a head start...

Pots of fun

Keep old supplement tubs handy and make up several days' worth of feed in one go, perhaps at the weekend or on your day off. Being late for work or school will soon be a thing of the past!

Hay fever!

Buy seven haynets – one for each day of the week – and fill them at the weekend or on your day off so that you can grab and run in the mornings. Store them in the feed room or hay barn, away from prying mouths.

Super sacks!

Old builders' merchant sacks designed to hold sand or bricks are perfect for containing dirty bedding because they're strong, durable, hold twice as much as most wheelbarrows and are easy to wash and store. You can also carry your hay in one of these sacks to ensure it doesn't get blown around on a windy day and you have to spend extra time sweeping it all up!

Alternatively, push your wheelbarrow all the way into the stable, muck out, then place a sack over the top to stop bedding falling out or being blown around on your way to the muck heap.

QUICK T!P

PROTECTION RACKET
Use a cotton summer sheet under your horse's stable blanket/rug to protect it from grease and dirt – it's much easier to wash and dry than a thick quilted blanket/rug.

Fashionably early

What a pair of old overalls or sweatpants/trackies and T-shirt lack in style they more than make up for in practicality – especially when you're rushing to get to work or get the kids to school. Worn over your daytime clothes, they can make the difference between you dashing home to change and being late for work or squashing your daytime clothes into a bag and looking creased and crumpled for that important business meeting!

Machine clean

Investing in synthetic saddlery for the winter can really cut down on cleaning time and means you can keep your best leather tack for the summer shows. Especially popular with endurance riders, synthetic saddlery requires much less care than leather and can be washed or brushed clean. Alternatively, a webbing bridle can be washed in the clothes washer/ washing machine. Place it in an old pillowcase first, though, so that the buckles don't clank against the sides of the washer or get stuck in the drum. You can wash fabric girths in the same way – or knot an old sock onto each end to protect both the buckles and your washer.

QUICK T!P

SHINE ON!
Running metal items like bits, spurs and stirrup irons through a dishwasher cycle will make them look like new!

Handy hint

Keep your hands clean and prevent sore, chapped skin and broken nails by storing a box of disposable gloves in the tack room. Wear a pair while mucking out or applying creams/lotions so you don't have to spend time washing your hands afterwards.

Shake 'n stir!

Shake some talcum powder into your horse's boots to keep his legs cleaner and drier, plus a puff of powder into your long boots will enable you to pull them on and off easier.

Getting the needle

When braiding/plaiting your horse for a show, thread several needles in advance and pin them into the front of your T-shirt so they're to hand and you don't lose them.

Winter warmers

Those long dark, cold winter nights don't mean you and your horse have to hibernate – thanks to a bit of forward planning and the following tips, you can keep both busy and sane…

Spring into action

If you plan to compete your horse the following spring or summer, winter is the time to expand your knowledge. The dark evenings are ideal for curling up on the couch and studying training DVDs. Alternatively, check the Internet or your local riding schools/training establishments for any evening lecture demos, or devise a winter schooling plan with set training goals to keep both you and your horse motivated until spring.

N'ice idea

In snowy weather, use petroleum jelly to grease the inside of your horse's hooves to prevent balling.

No sweat!

When returning from a wet, muddy and cold ride, don't allow your sweaty horse to stand for long without a blanket/rug. Invest in either a wicking blanket/rug or a breathable cooler to dry him off and keep him warm at the same time.

Inside out

Soak hay in a barn or shed so it does not freeze.

Switched on

Always ensure you have a flashlight/torch – and some spare batteries – handy when you are at the stables in poor light. Plus, you never know when there may be a power failure.

Chill out!

Sheepskin saddle pads/numnahs are useful for cold-backed horses sensitive to chilly conditions.

Ground control

Putting down used bedding – shavings are particularly good – in saturated field gateways can help soak up some of the wetness and prevent the ground from becoming even muddier.

But for a more long-term solution, try laying bark chippings or some form of hardcore such as specialized plastic or rubber matting/chopped rubber or asphalt scalpings (pieces of leftover crumbled road material) around the gate area. This may also help to prevent mud fever, especially if your horse and his field mates tend to loiter around the gate at feed time or before they are brought in.

All wrapped up

During particularly cold spells, an old duvet is excellent for use under a blanket/rug to add extra warmth without weight. In addition, they're easy to clean and don't harbor parasites. Also, if you have a thin-skinned horse that feels the cold more, don't under-estimate the benefits of bandaging his legs – not too tightly, though – at night.

Banding together

If your blankets/rugs don't already have them, put a rubber washer or a couple of rubber bands around the T-clips on your blankets/rugs, to keep them done up.

Age old problem

If you own an elderly equine, put a blanket/rug on him as soon as the weather starts to get nippy as veterans are more prone to losing condition in the cold. And allow him more time to warm up on cold mornings before asking him to work properly.

Cut and dried

Using a coat conditioner (not on the saddle area though!) will help mud slide off your horse, while applying a de-tangler lotion to your horse's tail will mean mud and muck is a lot easier to brush out, especially if you're in a rush or off to a competition.

Instead of washing off a muddy horse, especially in cold conditions, bandage straw around his legs and place a layer under a cooler or wicking blanket/rug, then brush off dried mud later.

Alternatively, paint liquid paraffin on your horse's legs before he's turned out so mud can be hosed or brushed off more easily when he's brought in.

And putting your horse's mane into long braids/plaits will attract a lot less mud from the field.

Having a ball

To prevent water from completely icing over in freezing conditions, place a football or tennis ball in troughs and buckets. Keep a hammer and colander or large sieve/sifter handy in case you need to break and remove the ice.

Salt wash

If your barn/yard uses salt on concrete areas to keep ice at bay, remember to wash off your horses' hooves regularly as the salt will dry them out.

Harrowing salt into your arena can prevent it from freezing over, plus don't forget to treat the steps and top surface of your mounting block, if you use one.

Alternatively, mucking out bedding straight from the stable into the yard area helps melt ice the natural way but remove droppings first!

Cough mixture

If your horse tends to pick up a cough during the winter months, try mixing half a teaspoon of powdered mustard into each feed – an old wives' tale that some owners swear by!

The heat is on

No heat in your tack room to dry out wet outdoor blankets/rugs overnight? Then try draping them over a suspended or elevated jump pole or old broom handle, with the lining side uppermost, to prevent the weight of the water and mud draining through to the lining. Failing that, braid/plait some baler twine and hang it across the tack room or drape rugs across a corner.

QUICK T!P
DOWN THE DRAIN!
Check and unblock the drains at your stables regularly as straw and shavings can clog them up and cause a flood during heavy rain.

Ski lift!

There are no prizes for looking glamorous or fashionable around the barn/ yard, particularly when temperatures plunge. For carrying out mundane stable duties such as mucking out or clipping, try a pair of old ski salopettes (quilted trousers that reach your chest and are held up by shoulder straps) – ask at your nearest ski hire shop for ex-rental ones – they can be a godsend for keeping you both clean and warm!

Freeze factors

Chain harrowing the surface of an outdoor arena just before a hard frost will prevent it from taking hold. Remember that if trees overshadow your arena, rays from any winter sun will be unable to melt the frost evenly – so avoid those frozen areas.

Looking on the outside?

Winter can be a good time to buy a horse because if you can cope with this time of year, the rest is a breeze!

If you're after a type of horse/pony that has adapted to the British/Irish climate and can cope with living out all-year-round in the tough winter weather conditions, then native breeds (such as the Scottish Highland, Welsh ponies and Irish Connemara) and cobs are ideal. Their chunkier bodies and shorter legs conserve heat better while their thick coats and long manes and tails have evolved to retain warmth. Plus their larger heads allow more space to warm the air as it is inhaled, and their small ears minimize heat loss.

Meanwhile, if you're more interested in a horse/pony that's better suited to a warmer climate, consider a thinner-skinned, finer-coated, longer-eared breed like a full- or part-bred Arab or Thoroughbred. They have evolved in hot, dry weather conditions, and their bodies are better adapted to cooling them down rather than warming them up.

Leap into action

Take advantage of winter to brush up on your and your horse's techniques so you're in tiptop physical and mental shape come the spring. Use the time to focus on your long term aims, ensuring the basics are secure, introduce new exercises and work on improving your position and your horse's outline and way of going.

Here are four suggested exercises…

1. Smaller loops and circles to improve your horse's obedience, balance and suppleness – ride this exercise in walk, rising trot, sitting trot and canter, and with an advanced horse, you can introduce flying changes

2. Serpentine loops of 3m or 5m to aid suppleness – once you've mastered this, introduce some halt transitions over the centre line to vary the exercise

3. Short diagonal lines – frequent changes of rein in walk or trot helps develop flexibility

4. Shortening and lengthening strides on 20m circles – ride in walk, trot and canter to help engage your horse and develop more scope in his paces.

Get packing!

If you're heading to a winter competition, remember to pack some snacks and hot drinks to keep your energy levels up; a warm jacket; spare socks; thick gloves; waterproofs and a shovel and some old sacks in case you get bogged down if the car park is in a muddy field or on wet grass.

A handwarmer, which you squeeze to activate – available from a saddler or pharmacy – can be a lifesaver!

Clear vision

If competing in an indoor arena, remember to allow your horse's eyes time to adjust when going from natural light into a brightly-lit area.

Lighter layer

Keep yourself warm by wearing pantyhose/a pair of tights – or silk gloves, socks and undershirt/vest/singlet – underneath your normal riding clothes. A thin layer underneath is more insulating and less bulky than two thick layers.

Alternatively, a polythene food or plastic bag worn between two pairs of socks will help insulate your feet, especially if you're wearing rubber boots. And a cotton headscarf under your riding helmet will keep your ears warm – but you'll still be able to hear the traffic if hacking out.

Going barefoot

Is your horse looking forward to a winter holiday? If he's out of work for a month or less, it might be cost-effective to ask the farrier to remove his hind shoes. If you're not planning to ride your horse for a longer period, it's often more economical to have both front and hind shoes taken off.

Hot stuff!

While summer offers the best riding opportunities, the hot weather can have downsides. Here's my summer survival guide…

Sense and sensitivity

Stock up on supplies of high protection sunscreen if a period of hot weather is forecast – especially if you have a gray horse. Grays and horses with pink noses are more susceptible to sunburn.

Life's a beach

Lucky enough to live near the beach? Then take extra care with your tack after a ride as salt water dries up leather and rots stitching – rinse well with clean fresh water and leave it to dry naturally.

Fly byes!

If flies bother you while you're on board, spray some equine insect repellent over your riding helmet.

Buzz off!

Ward off those pesky summer insects with a home-made fly repellent, which can be just as effective as many expensive preparations available in saddleries and tack shops. Always try on a small patch of your horse's skin first to check there's no adverse reaction to the mixture:

Concoction 1:   16 fl oz (US) or 1 pint (UK) of cold stewed tea; 16 fl oz/1 pint of vinegar; fresh garlic oil; several drops of lavender, tea tree, clove and rosemary oils.

Concoction 2:   Mix a few drops of sandalwood and eucalyptus oils with liquid paraffin, liquid soap and water.

Concoction 3:   A solution comprising two-parts lemon juice, four-parts vinegar and four-parts cold tea.

Concoction 4:   Mix two tablespoons of denatured alcohol (methylated spirits), one tablespoon of dishwashing (washing up) liquid, four tablespoons of vinegar and 8 fl oz/half a pint of strong tea – fill up with water to two liters and use as a spray.

Concoction 5:   Rinse the mane and tail with two tablespoons of cider vinegar to one liter/33 fl oz/two pints of water.

Bug barriers

If flies are still getting under your horse's skin, try:

- Mixing garlic in his drinking water or giving one clove of garlic a day in feed, building up to four or five cloves daily – you'll find that this will ward off most insects (and everything else, come to that!)

- Siting muck heaps as far away from stables and grazing as possible, and removing droppings from stables and fields as often as you can

- Providing a field shelter for your horse – he's more likely to use it in summer to avoid the flies than he is to get out of bad weather in winter

- Putting up strips of flypaper in stables, ensuring that they're out of your horse's reach

- Using a fly sheet or cotton summer sheet to keep your horse comfortable

- Attaching a fly fringe to your horse's halter/headcollar (either a leather or special safety one so it'll break/pull apart if it gets caught) or a fly net/mask/hood, which covers his face and/or muzzle

- Applying a fine layer of oil such as petroleum jelly to the surface of your horse's skin twice daily, which will help prevent flies from landing and therefore feeding

- Sponging your horse thoroughly after exercise so flies aren't attracted to his sweaty coat

- Using an equine shampoo containing a mild antiseptic or insect repellent when bathing your horse

- Avoiding areas where flies congregate, such as fields with droppings, water or woods, as well as at dusk when there are more insects about

- Attaching a few crushed stalks of elder to the browband of your horse's bridle while out riding.

Money Matters

> **" A stubborn horse walks behind you. An impatient horse walks in front of you, but a noble horse walks with you. "**

Monty Roberts

Chapter 9
Money Matters

Owning a horse is a big drain on anyone's bank account. Here are a few ways of cutting costs without cutting corners...

Where there's muck...

Unwanted, old or damaged plastic laundry baskets can come in useful as ideal 'muck lugs' or skips for mucking out your horse – plus they are just a fraction of the price of 'proper' items bought new.

Flawless flooring

Rubber matting can be a really good way of saving on bedding costs in the long run, especially if you stable your horse on shavings. Instead of using a bale of shavings every other day, rubber matting can help cut this down to around one bale per fortnight. Plus it helps cushion horses with sore joints and can speed up your daily chores – mucking out five stables can take just 25 minutes!

QUICK T!P
IT'S A WRAP!
Old towels come in really useful for rubbing down your horse when he returns sweaty from a ride.

Smooth as silk

To prevent blanket/rug rubs, use an old piece of silk or satin and sew it into the inside shoulders of your blankets/rugs, rather than buying more expensive purpose-made shoulder protectors.

In the frame

A folding drying rack/clothes horse is a great winter investment for your tack room – a cheap but practical drier for lightweight items such as boots and saddle pads/numnahs.

Secondhand savings

Instead of discarding worn-out blankets/rugs, keep them to patch up future tears and holes, or for replacing or repairing buckles, straps and fillet strings.

Added benefits

Sunflower oil from supermarkets is a cheap, long-lasting, slow-releasing supplement, high in protein. It keeps the gut moving and gives the coat a healthy shine.

Cod liver oil, which is good for condition and healthy joints because it contains high levels of omega-3 fatty acids and vitamins A and D, is cheaper when bought in a large gallon (or four liter) tin. Why not split the cost with a friend at the stables?

Keep in shape

Instead of throwing away old saddle soap tins, nail them to your tack room wall as bridle pegs. They're just the size to keep leather crownpieces/headstalls or headpieces of bridles, halters/headcollars and longe/lunge cavessons in shape and to prevent cracking.

Take three…

… baked bean cans, remove the labels and ends from two (plus just one end from the third) and nail them to your tack room wall. Leave about four inches between each one and hey presto! Now you have a fantastic whip tidy for schooling and longe/lunge whips.

Getting the boot

Keep your leather riding boots in tiptop condition by using large plastic soft drink bottles filled with water as cheap but effective boot shapers/trees.

Going green

Call into your local produce market, greengrocer or farmer's market and ask if you can have – or buy cheaply – left-over carrots, apples, beetroot, swedes, parsnips or turnips at the end of the day. Just check none are moldy, and cut them lengthways into 'fingers' before giving them sparingly to your horse in his feed. In fact, some owners believe that a large turnip,

swede or parsnip left in their horse's manger or hidden in his haynet for him to nibble at is good for helping to relieve boredom in the stable.

Cost shavings!

Limit wastage when mucking out by sieving clean shavings through an old plastic laundry or washing basket back onto the bed.

In a scrape?

Hot day, sweaty horse? No sweat scraper? Improvise by using a double length of baler twine drawn across your horse's coat to remove excess moisture following exercise or a bath.

Group practice

Encourage everyone at your barn/yard to club together and buy wormers in bulk, thus saving between 5 and 10 per cent – plus many companies offer free delivery with big orders, too.

Just bootiful!

If you can't afford a new pair of leather boots for the show ring, either buy secondhand ones or splash out on a top quality pair of rubber ones and ask a saddler to stitch garter straps on them for a professional look.

It's a scoop!

Cut diagonally across large plastic soft drink bottles to create home-made feed scoops.

D-I-Y waterproofing

If the seams of your outdoor blankets/rugs leak during wet weather, rub candle wax along the stitching.

" **Whoever said money can't buy happiness didn't know where to buy a horse.** "

Anon

In the clear

Clear plastic duvet bags with a zip are ideal for storing blankets/rugs when they're not in use.

Pole work

Broken poles can be cut down and used as rails for stiles (narrow show jumps) or for marking out the edges of a schooling arena in a flat field.

All sewn up

Save the D-rings off old blankets/rugs or discarded items of tack and sew them onto an outdoor blanket/rug as a neck cover attachment. That way you won't need to go to the expense of buying a brand new blanket/rug with either a detachable neck cover or a 'combo' design. Neck covers are great for keeping horses warm and clean in winter – and for saving you grooming time.

Fishing around!

Mend your blankets/rugs by using nylon fishing line or dental floss – strong, durable and waterproof!

Hand wash!

Instead of splashing out on a professional blanket/rug cleaning service, wash your horse's blankets/rugs yourself in a large garbage can/dustbin or old bath, using hypo-allergenic washing liquid and a pole!

With outdoor blankets/rugs, hang them over a gate and use a pressure washer to blast off all traces of mud and muck.

Cold case

Old chest freezers make great rodent-proof feed bins or storage containers for gear you want to keep clean and dry. For safety, disable the locking mechanism first, though.

Treading the boards

For a home-made portable mounting block, nail a flat sheet of wood onto the bottom of an old milk crate, to make it safe and more sturdy.

Sleeping partner

Turn an old sleeping bag into a warm quilted stable blanket/rug by removing the zip, cutting out a semi-circular section at one end for the neck and shoulders and stitching around the edges. Strips of broad Velcro make excellent breast straps.

Shopping around

Top quality show jackets, shirts (boys' school shirts are especially good for this) and colorful ties can be bought for the show ring from charity shops at a fraction of the price.

QUICK T!P
PEDAL POWER
Bicycle puncture repair kits can be used as a quick-fix solution for mending holes in rubber riding boots. The job won't look pretty but at least you won't have to shell out for a new pair and your feet will stay dry!

A clean sweep

A handy – and cheap – way of hanging blankets/rugs is to use an old broom handle. Simply tie a length of baler twine at each end and secure it to the top of the bars of the stable at the desired height. Remember to hang blankets/rugs with the innerside uppermost so that the water and mud soak outwards, not inwards into the lining. And bring wet outdoor blankets/rugs inside overnight if the temperature is very cold, to prevent them from freezing and to give them a chance to dry out and air.

Five of the Best

Here is the author's pick of the world's best sports horse and rider combinations over recent years...

Dressage

1. **Moorlands Totilas**, nicknamed '**Toto**', is widely recognized as the most outstanding competitive dressage horse in the world today, commanding a cult following and being branded an equine rock star.

   The 11-year-old 17.1hh Dutch Warmblood stallion by Gribaldi became the first horse to score above 90 per cent. With **Edward Gal**, the pair were the first to win three gold medals at the 2010 FEI World Equestrian Games. The horse is now partnered by **Matthias Alexander Rath**.

2. When German rider **Nicole Uphoff** won her first international dressage event aboard the brilliant Westphalian **Rembrandt** in 1987, it was the start of her dominance of the sport for the next 10 years.

   The pair competed at the 1988 Seoul, 1992 Barcelona and 1996 Atlanta Olympics, winning individual and team gold in the latter two.

3. At just 20 years of age, **Laura Bechtolsheimer** became the youngest British Dressage National Champion in 2005.

   Aboard her top horse **Mistral Hojris**, or '**Alf**', a 16-year-old 17hh chestnut Danish-bred gelding by Michellino, Laura surpassed her personal best scores and achieved three British international Grand Prix records and three silver medals at the 2010 FEI World Equestrian Games in Kentucky.

4. German dressage rider **Isabell Werth** is best known for riding Hanoverian gelding **Gigolo** to victory in countless Olympics, World and European Championships between 1992 and 2000.

   The pairing won four Olympic gold medals and two silver, four World Championships, eight European Championships and four German titles.

5. Dutch rider **Anky van Grunsven** lit up the dressage scene at the 2000 Olympics, winning gold with Oldenburg gelding **Bonfire** and claiming nine World Cup dressage championships (five with Bonfire and four with **Salinero**). Anky also won gold at both the 2004 and 2008 Olympics with Salinero.

    Bonfire was a consistent and talented performer who boasted lightness, elegance, enthusiasm and athleticism in equal measure, making the sport look easy.

Showjumping

1. Originally known as Battle Boy, Irish sports horse **Boomerang** is synonymous with the Hickstead Derby, winning the illustrious competition an unsurpassed four times from 1976 to 1979.

    The 16.2hh bay gelding was piloted to his many victories first by Liz Edgar and Paul Schockemohle and then most famously at Hickstead by **Eddie Macken**.

2. Three-time individual European showjumping champion **Deister** was partnered to his many victories by top German rider **Paul Schockemohle**.

    The bay Hanoverian gelding was undoubtedly Schockemohle's best horse and commanded a loyal following during the 1980s, winning five German Championships, two Hickstead Derbys, the King George V Gold Cup and team bronze at the 1984 Los Angeles Olympics.

3. First called Winston after the wartime British prime minister, it's hard to believe that World Champion showjumper **Big Ben** grew to 17.3hh when his dam was just 15hh.

    The Belgian-bred horse was first sold to a buyer in Holland before being bought for Canadian showjumper **Ian Millar** to ride.

This proved a formidable partnership with Millar and Big Ben notching up more than 40 Grand Prix victories including six Spruce Meadows Derbys, two consecutive World Cup Finals – the first horse to achieve this – and $1.5m in prize money.

4. Olympic gold and silver medalists **Eric Lamaze** and **Hickstead** have formed a formidable showjumping partnership over the last 10 years.

   The 16hh bay Dutch Warmblood stallion and Canadian Lamaze were members of the winning Nations Cup team in 2006, won team silver and individual gold at the 2008 Olympics and jumped four clear rounds at the 2010 World Equestrian Games, earning Hickstead the title Best Horse in the discipline.

5. American-born showjumper **Meredith Michaels-Beerbaum** trained with Paul Schockemohle before buying her own training center and switching nationalities when she married German showjumper Markus Beerbaum, brother of Ludger.

   Together with **Shutterfly**, Meredith won the 2003 Olympia Grand Prix, silver at the 2004 World Cup Final, gold at the 2005, 2008 and 2009 World Cup Finals (the first woman to win this three times) and was the first woman to top the FEI showjumping world rankings in 2004.

Eventing

1. New Zealand-born event rider **Mark Todd** CBE was voted Rider of the 20th Century by the FEI.

   'Toddy' won gold medals at the 1984 and 1988 Olympics not to mention Burghley five times and Badminton – the pinnacle of the sport in the UK – four times (he was the oldest rider at 55 to win the event in 2011).

   He also won the World Championships in 1990 and 1998, the European Championships in 1997 and other international events and team and individual titles too numerous to mention.

   His most famous horse was **Charisma**, a 15.2hh Thoroughbred with a dash of Percheron blood.

2. Following in his countryman Mark Todd's footsteps by announcing a return to the sport from retirement, **Blyth Tait** is one of only four New Zealanders to compete at four Olympics and win four medals.

   Tait won individual and team gold at the 1990 World Equestrian Games aboard **Messiah**, individual bronze and team silver at the 1992 Olympics riding **Latta**, individual gold and team bronze at the 1996 Olympics and double World Championship gold in 1998 on **Ready Teddy**.

3. Regarded as America's most prolific international event rider and breeder, **Bruce Davidson** first became a member of the US equestrian team in 1971. He won Olympic team gold in 1976 and 1984, Olympic team silver in 1972 and 1996 and became the first American to win the World Championships at Burghley in 1974 as well as winning back-to-back World Championships at Kentucky in 1978.

   In addition to competing at four Olympic Games, he rode round Badminton seven times, becoming the first American to win this prestigious event in 1995 on **Eagle Lion**.

4. Formerly Lucinda Prior-Palmer, **Lucinda Green** MBE won Badminton a record six times on six different horses – **Be Fair** (1973), **Wideawake** (1976), **George** (1977), **Killaire** (1979), **Regal Realm** (1983) and **Beagle Bay** (1984).

   First representing Britain at the 1973 European Championships, she was European Champion in 1975 and 1977 and won Burghley in 1981, team gold at the World Championships in 1982, team and individual silver at the 1983 European Championships and team silver at the 1984 Olympics.

5. Born Virginia Helen Antoinette Holgate in Malta, **Ginny Leng** (now **Elliot**) was a UK eventing heroine during the 1980s.

   Ginny won the individual European eventing title on three consecutive occasions – 1985, 1987 and 1989 – a feat never matched before or since. Her top horses were **Priceless**, **Night Cap** and **Master Craftsman**.

Glossary

ACTION	the movement of a horse's skeletal frame as it goes from one place to the next.
AIDS	the signals made by the rider or driver to communicate his or her wishes to the horse. Natural aids are the hands, legs, bodyweight and voice, while artificial aids include whips and spurs.
BALER OR BALING TWINE	sisal or synthetic string used to bind hay and straw, which comes in handy for various yard tasks, not least in the safe tying up of horses.
BARGING	a stable vice or bad habit that involves a horse running over its handler, usually due to fright or bad manners, in a narrow or confined space or when being lead.
BETWEEN HAND AND LEG	when the horse is engaged and pushing forward from behind and the rider has a contact on the reins, ensuring that the horse is connected and 'on the bit'.
BOMBPROOF	a horse that is calm, safe, confident and obedient to ride in all situations due to having been exposed – and is therefore de-sensitized – to a variety of scary stimuli.
BONE	the measurement taken around the cannon bone below the knee, which affects the horse's ability to carry weight.
BOW HOCKS	outward-turned hock joints, a conformational fault.

BOX WALKER   a stable vice or bad habit that involves the horse continuously walking round its stable in circles, usually caused by boredom or stress.

BOXY FEET   hooves that are 'boxed in' and upright with closed instead of open heels.

BREED   an equine group whose members have been selectively bred for consistent characteristics over a period of time and with pedigrees recorded in a stud book.

BRUSHING   when a horse's hoof or shoe strikes the inside of the opposite leg at or near the fetlock due to poor conformation or action.

COLD-BACKED   a horse that shows symptoms of back pain such as dipping away or putting its back up.

COLDBLOOD   generic term for heavy European equine breeds descended from a prehistoric horse.

COLT   an uncastrated male horse under four years of age.

CONCENTRATES   also referred to as hard feed or straights in the UK, includes grains (whole, rolled, crushed or cracked), sweet feed (grain mixed with molasses), and manufactured feeds (pellets, cubes or extruded).

CONFORMATION   a horse's physical build; the way it is 'put together' in terms of its bone structure, musculature and body proportions and their relation to each other.

COW HOCKS	opposite conformational fault to bow hocks, this is when a horse's hocks turn inwards like a cow's.
CRIB-BITING	a stable vice or habit that involves the horse grabbing the edge of an object such as a stable door with its incisor teeth and gradually gnawing at it, usually caused by boredom or from copying another horse's behavior.
DISHED PROFILE	typical of breeds like the Arab, this is a concave head profile.
DISHING	refers to the action of a horse's foreleg when the toe is thrown outwards in a circular movement.
EWE NECK	a neck that is concave along its upper edge resulting in protruding muscular development on the underside.
FEI	abbreviation for Federation Equestre Internationale (International Equestrian Federation), the governing body of international equestrian sport.
FILLY	a female horse under four years of age.
FOREHAND	the part of the horse in front of the rider – the head, neck, shoulders, withers and forelegs.
GAIT	one of the different ways in which a horse can move, such as walk, trot and canter, either naturally or as a result of training.
GELDING	a castrated male horse.
GRAND PRIX	the highest level in the sport of dressage, which requires the execution of the most difficult moves

such as piaffe, flying changes, passage, pirouette and half pass. Also refers to the highest level of showjumping, where the horse jumps an internationally ranked course of 10 to 16 obstacles, with heights and spreads of up to 6.5ft (2m).

HACKING	a term commonly used in the UK, Canada and the eastern US to describe riding a horse out for light exercise; this is more commonly known as trail riding in the western US.
HAND	a unit of measurement (one hand equals four inches or 10cm) to describe a horse's height.
HAUTE ECOLE	the classical art of advanced equitation.
HEAD CARRIAGE	the way a horse carries its head, such as in a rounded shape for dressage or long and low for Western pleasure.
HEAVY HORSE	any large draught/draft horse, such as the Shire or Percheron.
HINDQUARTERS	describes the part of the horse lengthways from the rear of the flank to the beginning of the tail and downwards to the top of the second thigh.
HOGGING	the removal of a horse's mane for appearance, such as cobs to show off their muscular necks, or with polo ponies for practical/safety reasons.
HOLLOW BACK	this conformational fault, also known as a 'sway back', is when a horse's shape between its withers and loins is concave.
HOTBLOOD	an Arab or Thoroughbred.

HOT UP	a horse that becomes over-excited is said to 'hot up'.
LIGHT OF BONE	a conformational fault referring to insufficient bone below the knee to support both the horse and rider's bodyweight without strain, limiting the animal's weight carrying capacity.
MANEGE	a schooling arena for training or exercising horses.
MARE	a female horse aged four or more years.
PACE	a way of describing how a horse moves, be it walk, trot, canter or gallop. Also refers to a two-beat lateral gait with the legs on the same side of the horse moving together at the same time. American Standardbreds are harness raced at the pace, as are Icelandic Horses under saddle.
PEDIGREE	the details of ancestry recorded in a breed stud book.
PIGEON TOES	a conformational fault where the feet point inwards.
PLAITING	a faulty action where the feet are placed in front of each other.
POINTS	a horse's external features that make up its conformation.
QUICK RELEASE KNOT	used to avoid injury, this safety knot is employed when tying and restraining a horse and can be undone quickly in an emergency, even when a horse is pulling back.
RIDING HORSE	as opposed to a draught/draft or carriage horse, an animal that has conformation and action suitable for riding.

ROACH BACK	a convex curvature of the horse's spine between its withers and loins – a conformational fault.
ROMAN PROFILE OR ROMAN NOSE	a convex head profile associated with primitive breeds, especially coldblood heavy horses.
SCHOOLMASTER	a horse unlikely to be less than 12 or 13 years old that has the experience and ability to help a rider learn and perfect certain skills.
SCLERA	the outer membrane of the eyeball.
SHORT OF A RIB	a conformational fault of slack loins, caused by too wide a space between the point of the hip and the last rib.
SICKLE HOCKS	too strongly angled hocks when viewed from the side, a conformational fault that can cause hindleg weakness.
STALLION	an uncastrated or 'entire' male horse aged four years or more.
STUD BOOK	a book kept by a breed society where the pedigrees of purebred horses are recorded.
SWAN NECK	a conformational fault whereby a horse's upper neck curves upwards so that the head joins it in an almost vertical line, which can affect movement.
TACK	equipment used for riding and driving.
TOPLINE	the upper curvature of a horse's withers, back and loins.
TWITCH	a device used to restrain horses during stressful situations such as veterinary treatment or clipping.

It consists of a stick-like handle loop of chain or rope on the end or a metal ring with a rope loop wrapped around the upper lip of the horse and tightened. It works by triggering the release of endorphins from the horse's brain, producing a calming effect. A 'humane' twitch is a plier-like clamp that squeezes the lip in a nutcracker motion.

TYPE	horses that fulfil a particular purpose, such as a hack, hunter or cob, but do not belong to a specific breed.
WARMBLOOD	this generally refers to half- or part-bred horses, usually the result of Thoroughbred or Arab crosses with other blood.
WEAVING	a stable vice or bad habit whereby the horse shifts its weight from one leg to another, swaying its head and neck from side to side, which is usually caused by boredom but can also be learned from other horses.
WELL-SPRUNG RIBS	long rounded ribs that offer plenty of room for the lungs to work efficiently and provide a comfortable seat for the rider.
WHORL	a patch of hair growing in the opposite direction to the rest of the coat.
WINDSUCKING	a stable vice or bad habit associated with crib-biting. While grasping the edge of an object such as a stable door with its incisor teeth, the horse will arch its neck, pull back and suck air into its stomach, often making a noise.

Bob Langrish MBE
EQUESTRIAN PHOTOGRAPHER

All the photographs in this book are by **Bob Langrish MBE**. Bob has established a firm reputation as one of the foremost international equestrian photographers in the world. After 38 years of specialization in this field, he has built an equestrian photographic library of over 400,000 pictures covering all aspects of the horse. He has taken photographs at six Olympic games and travels to the United States of America at least seven times a year. He works for top equestrian magazines in more than 20 countries around the world.

Index